William John Lofite

Windsor Castle

With a Description of the Park, Town and Neighbourhood. Jubilee Edition

William John Lofite

Windsor Castle
With a Description of the Park, Town and Neighbourhood. Jubilee Edition

ISBN/EAN: 9783744717182

Printed in Europe, USA, Canada, Australia, Japan

Cover: Foto ©ninafisch / pixelio.de

More available books at **www.hansebooks.com**

Jubilee Edition

WINDSOR CASTLE

With a Description of the Park, Town, and Neighbourhood

By

W. J. LOFTIE, B.A., F.S.A.

Author of 'A History of London,' 'Memorials of the Savoy,' &c. &c.

LONDON
SEELEY & CO. 46, 47, & 48 ESSEX STREET, STRAND
1887

All rights reserved

Dedicated

BY SPECIAL PERMISSION

TO HER MOST GRACIOUS MAJESTY

QUEEN VICTORIA

CONTENTS.

I.—GENERAL VIEW.

Windsor Castle and the Tower of London compared—The Geographical Situation of Windsor—Origin of the Name—The Mound—The Manor of Clewer—Windsor Castle a Half Hide in Clewer—The Descendants of the Conqueror at Windsor—New Windsor—The Honour of Windsor—The Constable—The Environs—The Scenery of the Park—The Picturesque Aspect of the Castle—Wyatville . . . 1

II.

Edward the Confessor at Old Windsor—Forged Deeds—The Grant to Westminster—William the Conqueror at New Windsor—The Norman Castle—Henry I.—The Constables—Wars of John—The Braoses—Magna Charta—Henry III.—His Buildings—His Treachery to the Citizens of London . 23

III.

A Tournament—Birth of Edward III.—Renovation of the Castle—The Round Tower and the Round Table—Royal Prisoners—The Founders of the Order of the Garter—The Death of Philippa—Richard II. at Windsor—His Farewell to Queen Isabel—Plot at Windsor against Henry IV.—James of Scotland—The Heart of St. George—Birth of Henry VI.—Edward IV.—His Body Examined—Visit of the King of Castile—Henry VIII.—The Earl of Surrey—Burial-place of Henry VIII. and Queen Jane Seymour 49

IV.

Early Views of the Castle—Queen Elizabeth's *Boethius*—Norden's View—The Dragon's Fountain—James I.—Old Descriptions—The Parliamentary Army—Charles I. a Prisoner—His Burial—Examination of his Remains in 1813—Cromwell at Windsor—The Alterations under Charles II.—The Star Building—Pepys at Windsor—The Pope's Nuncio—The Duke of Gloucester's Death—Improvements under William III.—Queen Anne. 78

V.

George III. at Windsor—Madame d'Arblay's 'Diary'—Her Short Sight—Topography of the Castle—The State Apartments—The Queen's Lodge—Court Life—Herschel—Discomfort of the House—The King's Illness—Queen Charlotte at Frogmore—James Wyatt—Sir Jeffry Wyatville—His Merits and Faults as an Architect—The 'Restoration' of Windsor Castle—Death of George IV. 104

VI.

The Chapel Royal of St. George—The Old Chapel of St. Edward—Wolsey's Tomb-house—The Sarcophagus—The Pope's Nuncio at Windsor—The Royal Vault—George the Third's Family—Positions of the Royal Coffins—Some Royal Funerals—The Prince Consort's Family Memorial—The Tomb-house Transformed—The Mausoleum at Frogmore—The First Chapel of St. George 128

VII.

The Chapel of Edward III.—The College—The Knights—Bishop Beauchamp—The New Chapel of St. George—Burials—Sir Reginald Bray—Description of the Vaulting—Some of the Monuments—George III. 'restores' the Chapel—West's Transparency—Willement's Improvements—Sir Gilbert Scott's Work—Notice of some remarkable Deans—Spalato—Matthew Wren 155

VIII.

The Town of New Windsor—First Signs of Life—An Unfree Town—Its Troubles—The Charter of Edward I.—The Guild of the Holy Trinity—Windsor in Shakespeare's Time—The Scenery of 'The Merry Wives'—The Town Hall—Sir Christopher Wren, M.P.—St. John's Church . . . 185

IX.

The Home Park—Herne's Oak—Datchet Mead—Datchet—Iver Church—Langley Church, Almshouses, and Library—Upton Church—Salt Hill—Eton College—Gray and Stoke Poges—Burnham Beeches—The Northern and the Southern Environs of Windsor contrasted 209

X.

The Great Park—The Long Walk—The Statue of George III.—View from Snow Hill—The Trees—Cumberland Lodge—The Sandbys—Virginia Water—The Ruins—Belvidere Wood—Bishopsgate—Holloway College—Ascot—The Church—The Race-Course—The Southern Environs of Windsor 239

XI.

The Antiquity of Windsor Castle as a Residence—A Storehouse of Works of Art—The State Apartments—The Private Apartments—The Library—The Gold Room—Old Furniture—The Long Corridor—The Dining Room—The Drawing Rooms—Edward III.'s Tower—General Gordon's Bible—Conclusion 264

ILLUSTRATIONS.

QUEEN VICTORIA. *From the Statue by J. E. Boehm, R.A.*	*Frontispiece*
WINDSOR CASTLE FROM ROMNEY LOCK	*Page* 5
THE ROUND TOWER FROM THE GARDEN OF THE DEAN AND CANONS	9
WINDSOR CASTLE FROM THE BROCAS	19
OLD WINDSOR CHURCH	27
THE CLOISTERS AND THE DEANERY	35
THE NORMAN GATEWAY	41
THE NORMAN GATE	43
THE HUNDRED STEPS	45
A BIT FROM THAMES STREET	47
THE LOWER WARD	53
INTERIOR OF THE GREAT HALL	55
SKETCH IN THE STEWARD'S ROOM	57
SECTION OF THE INTERIOR OF THE ROUND TOWER	59
THE KITCHEN COURT, WINDSOR CASTLE	61
HENRY VIII.'S GATE	73
KING JOHN'S TOWER	82
FIREPLACE IN THE LIBRARY	85
SKETCH OF WINDOW AND SHUTTER IN PRISON ROOM IN NORMAN TOWER	89

CONTENTS.

	Page
THE PORTCULLIS IN THE NORMAN TOWER	89
PRISON ROOM ABOVE THE NORMAN TOWER	93
ORIEL IN THE LIBRARY	101
WINDSOR CASTLE IN THE EIGHTEENTH CENTURY	105
STAIRCASE AND CORRIDOR IN THE ROUND TOWER	119
NORTH TERRACE AND WINCHESTER TOWER	122
ST. GEORGE'S CHAPEL	129
AN ANCIENT CORNER OF THE CLOISTERS	134
THE MEMORIAL CHAPEL FROM THE CLOISTERS	137
ONE BAY OF THE MEMORIAL CHAPEL	141
ALBERT MEMORIAL CHAPEL	145
INTERIOR OF THE MEMORIAL CHAPEL	149
ROYAL MAUSOLEUM	151
DUCHESS OF KENT'S MAUSOLEUM, FROGMORE	152
ENTRANCE TO THE HORSESHOE CLOISTER	159
ST. GEORGE'S CHAPEL: THE CHOIR AND STALLS	161
THE HASTINGS CHAPEL	165
THE BRAY CHAPEL AND OLIVER KING'S CHANTRY	169
THE ROYAL CLOSET	173
INTERIOR OF ST. GEORGE'S CHAPEL	177
GARGOYLES, ST. GEORGE'S CHAPEL	180
WINDSOR CASTLE FROM THE BERKSHIRE SHORE	181
THE CURFEW TOWER	188
WINDSOR CASTLE FROM THAMES STREET	195
BITS OF OLD MARKET STREET, WINDSOR	199
WINDSOR TOWN-HALL FROM THE HIGH STREET	202
DATCHET	210

CONTENTS.

	Page
ALMSHOUSES AT LANGLEY	215
VIEW FROM THE TERRACE OF THE CASTLE	219
LIBRARY AT LANGLEY	222
ETON COLLEGE	227
STOKE POGES CHURCH	231
GRAY'S TOMB	233
BURNHAM BEECHES	235
WINDSOR PARK	241
THE LONG WALK	245
WINDSOR PARK	249
CUMBERLAND LODGE	253
ARTIFICIAL RUINS AT VIRGINIA WATER	255
DEER IN WINDSOR PARK	259
THE CURFEW TOWER BEFORE RESTORATION	265
WEST END OF THE INNER CLOISTERS	267
THE CLOISTER GARTH	269
THE INNER CLOISTERS	270
THE STATE STAIRCASE	277
ST. GEORGE'S HALL	283
THE CORRIDOR	287
THE GREEN DRAWING-ROOM	291

WINDSOR.

I.

General View.

Windsor Castle and the Tower of London compared—The Geographical Situation of Windsor—Origin of the Name—The Mound—The Manor of Clewer—Windsor Castle a Half Hide in Clewer—The Descendants of the Conqueror at Windsor—New Windsor—The Honour of Windsor—The Constable—The Environs—The Scenery of the Park—The Picturesque Aspect of the Castle—Wyatville.

IT would be very easy to institute a comparison between Windsor Castle and the Tower of London. Both owe their origin to William the Conqueror; both figure in history as alternately places of imprisonment, fortresses, palaces, and finally as the site of royal tombs. But while the associations which connect themselves in our minds with the Tower of London are mainly of a gloomy character, those which group themselves round Windsor Castle are cheerful. There are, it is true, dark scenes in its history; sorrow is more inseparable from human life than joy. Windsor held many captives in the early years of its existence: Robert Mowbray, some time Earl of Northumberland, was imprisoned here by William Rufus, and died a prisoner after thirty years of confinement; and he was the first of many. But this is only one aspect of the history of the Castle, and it is not the common one. When we visit the stateliest palace in Europe we are more apt to think of the chapters of the Garter, of the entertainment of foreign potentates, of the tournaments and processions, of the royal marriages and royal christenings, than of prisoners, or deaths, or funerals. Windsor stands to English history in an ornamental light. The scenes enacted here have been scenes of high ceremonial, of splendour, of royal pomp and magnificence, which throw into the shade the more gloomy events. Nevertheless, they must not be ignored; and we must keep in mind that Windsor Castle was first a fortress and a palace afterwards, and also that among the stately ceremonials which have taken place in the Chapel of St. George have not unfrequently been royal funerals.

The situation of Windsor Castle is in itself

most happy. After we pass the Albert Memorial in Hyde Park, there is no elevation of equal height on the western road before we reach Windsor, at twenty-one miles distance. Unlike some of the hills in sight, such as Harrow or Hampstead, the eminence on which the Castle stands is formed of chalk, a fragment of the white range which seems to have strayed across the Thames into Berkshire, while south from it stretches the beautiful sandy district—covered in many places by ancient forest trees alternating with open, breezy heaths—which is known as Snow Hill and Cooper's Hill, Bagshot and Ascot. Over them all once extended the great Windsor Forest, 120 miles in circumference, through which Saxon and Norman kings hunted the deer, the wolf, and the wild boar. It is now almost all enclosed, but here and there a wild common or a hurst of old oaks remains to tell of its former state. As we pass northward through the Great Park, the hill rises steeply before us, and the Thames makes a great bend so as almost to surround it. This, according to most authorities, is the 'winding shore,' the 'Windesoveres' of Geoffrey Gaimar, the 'Winlesoren' of King Edward, the 'Windesores' of Domesday, the 'Windleshore' of

Henry III. The derivation is more than doubtful. The name was applied originally to Old Windsor only, and has, most probably, some connexion with the not very distant Windlesham, which is pronounced 'Winsham.' In Anglo-Saxon, 'windle' is a willow, and 'ofer' is a shore; but 'windle' may refer to the winding course of the Thames, and 'ofer' may have been softened into 'oure,' and eventually 'or.' There is a river or brook called the Windles, which runs into the Thames at Chertsey; but Chertsey is too far from Windsor to allow of the connexion which Harrison, in the 'Description of Britain' prefixed to his edition of Hollinshead, would appear to attempt. As we shall see a little farther on, no physical feature of the modern Windsor can be taken into account in stating these questions, because, though the name is borrowed from the neighbouring parish, the town and the castle really stand in Clewer.

Although, then, before the Norman Conquest the great chalk bluff in Clewer, which stood between the vast Berkshire forest and the Thames, had on it no royal palace and was flanked by no town, there is reason to believe that it was crowned by an earthwork of considerable importance. A similar

WINDSOR CASTLE FROM ROMNEY LOCK.

but smaller mound is close by across the river, and is known as Salt Hill, and a third is, or was not very long ago, a little farther east at Langley. In the early days of the Saxon occupation of England, each family was isolated. A general government grew up by degrees; but the first settlers' first business was to provide for their own safety, and the safety of their slaves and their cattle. For this purpose in some places they made moats, in some mounds, in some both moats and mounds. All alike were called 'buries.' The mound, says Mr. George Clark, in his exhaustive work on 'Mediaeval Military Architecture,' was not intended for the defence of a tribe or territory, nor for the accommodation of fighting men; it was the centre and defence of a private estate, for the residence of the lord and his household, and for the protection of his tenants. Such mounds are almost innumerable in England, and a large number of them were used by the Conqueror and his successors as sites for the keeps of their castles. The Saxon buildings were of wood, and have everywhere perished, though the earthworks which supported the palisades remain; and at Windsor, as at Arundel, the mound with its ditch appears to be the central feature of a plan consisting of two base courts, connected by the mound in the centre.

Of the early history of the holding or manor we know very little. It was among the possessions of the ill-fated Harold, and we may, perhaps, reckon him as its first royal resident; but at the time of the Domesday Survey, Clewer was the land of Radulphus, the son of Seifride, and its intermediate history, so far as documentary evidence is concerned, is a blank. We may, however, judging from the history of other places, make up a kind of working theory to fit it. The manor consisted, according to the Survey, of five hides. With Harold's other estates it became the property of the Conqueror, by whom it was granted, with a certain reservation, to Radulphus, who was probably a Norman, though the name of Ralph, as Professor Freeman has pointed out, was not unknown among the English. Seifride's name has a very English look, answering as it does to the modern German Sigfried; still it is safer, as we know so little, to assume that Ralph, the grantee of Clewer, 'came over with the Conqueror.' In the same Domesday Survey are two other mentions of Windsor; one of them is in the account of Drayton, a manor in the

THE ROUND TOWER, FROM THE GARDEN OF THE DEAN AND CANONS.

adjoining county, Buckinghamshire. Drayton, we read, was held from Lewin of Neweham, by a certain Radulphus, whose surname is given as 'Passaquam.' He was bound to provide two armed men for the guard at Windsor. It would be going too far to identify Ralph Passaquam with Ralph, the son of Seifride, still the connexion of the name with Windsor is, to say the least, curious. The other mention of Windsor relates to the history of a certain Azor, who had been a steward (dispensator) in the reign of Edward the Confessor. William sent a writ relating to him from Windsor.

When William granted the manor of Clewer to Ralph, he made, as I have said, a reservation. Harold had owned five hides, Ralph only held four and a half. King William kept the chalk hill, with its ancient earthworks, in his own hands. How much a hide was in Berkshire at that time I cannot tell; as a rule, however, we may reckon it at something under sixty acres, including the uncultivated land. If the earthwork covered about thirteen acres, it will be seen that there was very little land adjoining in the King's possession; but this did not matter, because he already owned the manor of Old Windsor, and by taking the 'bury' of the

Clewer manor from it, and making himself a castle and residence close to Old Windsor, he naturally gave his castle the name, not of the parish or manor in which it was actually situated, but that of the original royal residence close by from which he removed the court. From the first the new castle was called after the old palace. It was never Clewer Castle, always Windsor Castle. As Domesday says, after mentioning that Harold had five hides and Ralf has four and a half, 'et castellum de Windesores est in dimidio hida;' the Castle of Windsor is on the remaining half hide.

The royal residence thus founded is the subject of these chapters. It was destined to be the scene of many great events in our history. William had other and greater castles, yet, with the single exception of the Tower of London, none is so intimately connected with the fate of his descendants. In the eight hundred years that have passed since he reserved the half-hide in Clewer, and removed Windsor thither, it has been alternately their palace, their prison, and their burial-place. Strange to say, we hear little of it at any time as a fortress. It was twice besieged and once surrendered under John, and Edward I. improved its defences. But it was always much more a palace than a castle and it is by no means certain what kind of keep, if any, covered the central mound before the reign of Edward III. In the lapse of centuries Windsor grew greater almost year by year. The descendants of its founder appear in it as on a stage, sometimes in mighty state, sometimes in sorrow, sometimes in danger; and hither we shall see the bodies of many of them brought to a last resting-place. At Windsor Henry I. married his second wife, and Henry II. compared himself to an eagle pursued by his own offspring. Here John came when Magna Charta was signed; and here Edward III. was born. Here the first chapter of the oldest and noblest Order of European knighthood was held. Here the Black Prince married the Fair Maid of Kent, and Froissart saw the King mourning for Queen Philippa. David Bruce and James Stuart, kings of Scotland, were here imprisoned, and the young Earl of March, heir to the English crown. In spite of his father's gloomy foreboding, Henry VI. was born at Windsor, and passed every winter in the Castle while he was a child. His 'holy shade' lingers rather at Eton beyond the river than in his birth-place. Edward IV. is more conspicuous at Windsor. He made the beautiful chapel, and lies buried in it himself, the first of a long line of kings; but Richard III. brought hither the body of Henry VI., and the rivals rest side by side. Henry VII. vaulted the chapel, and built the Tomb House for himself, and though he is buried at Westminster, Henry VIII., his son, lies under his father's chapel at Windsor 'by his true and loving wife Queen Jane.' Cranmer, Ridley, and Latimer, were at Windsor on their last melancholy journey to their fiery martyrdom at Oxford. The great Elizabeth loved the place, and did not Shakespeare immortalise the 'Merry Wives of Windsor' at her Grace's express command? Her successor was often here, and made that strange character, Antonio de Dominis, Dean. One snowy afternoon in February, 1649, the 'White King's' headless body was laid without funeral rites in the grave of Henry VIII. Cromwell saved the Castle, and Dean Wren saved the records of the Garter, and Wren's more famous son built what are still the State apartments for Charles II. William III. was at Windsor when the poor boy, his nephew, the hope of the nation, celebrated his last birthday, and almost on the morrow sickened and died. Queen Anne pursued the deer in the Park in a one-horse chaise; and Cumberland, under the first Georges, retired to his ranger's lodge to sulk. Windsor was in decay when George III. made it his chief residence, and everyone remembers Madame D'Arblay's account of the discomfort endured by the royal family and their courtiers. George IV. lived in a lodge in the Park while Wyatville made the old Castle what it is now and gave it the outline so familiar to all Englishmen.

Besides the Castle itself, there is much in its immediate neighbourhood to engage the attention. It has long been the habit of topographical writers to mention the town of New Windsor with contempt. But, though not very beautiful, it is by no means to be despised. No town can be very ugly which has the Thames winding round it and the woods of the Great Park in the background. There are, it is true, not many pretty buildings, but Wren designed the Town Hall, and it is an excellent specimen of his style. Some modern rows of villas are not very pleasing, but now that Windsor has become practically a suburb of London, we cannot wonder. It takes less time to reach Windsor by train than it took to reach Kensington by road a hundred years ago. The neighbourhood of the

Great Park must always be a charm to attract sojourners; and little towns, which till lately were but hamlets and villages, are springing up all round it. It would not be easy at the present day to define the 'Honour of Windsor;' but a few centuries ago the words had a very distinct meaning, and all the country for many miles on both sides of the Thames was comprehended within its boundaries. The 'Castle Court' had jurisdiction from Maidenhead Bridge to Egham, taking in places as far north as Beaconsfield. On the south it extended to within two miles of Guildford, and comprised twenty-four parishes in Berkshire, seventeen in Buckinghamshire, and eighteen in Surrey; but the town of New Windsor was expressly excepted from it. The Constable of Windsor Castle had within the Honour a place 'of very great antiquity, honour, power, and pleasure, but of very little profit.' So wrote Sir Bulstrode Whitelock, in 1660, to Lord Mordaunt, whom Charles II. had appointed Constable. This great officer had jurisdiction as judge for trial of suits of any value arising within the Honour. He appointed a steward, or deputy, to hear and determine cases, and licensed attorneys to practise before him. Furthermore, he was Keeper of the Forest and had the care of vert and venison, and power to hunt as he thought fit, 'not prejudicing the King's pleasure.' There was a prison within the Castle called the 'Coalhouse,' to which he could commit offenders. He was allowed to use any lodgings or rooms in the Castle, 'whereof the King hath not present use.'

Such was the 'Honour of Windsor,' in the seventeenth century. A little earlier the Constable had even greater powers, and was the judge of felonies as well as offences against the game-laws. His court was held at the outer gate-house, and its records went back at least to the reign of Richard II.

It will be best in the following chapters not to stray so far afield as the utmost verge of the Honour, but to confine ourselves to the places which lie near at hand. It is easy, with Windsor as a centre, to make excursions to see some of the most pleasant landscapes in England. The view from Cooper's Hill is famous. It has the advantage of including the Castle, with a beautiful foreground of wood. Another well-known view is from the statue on Snow Hill, at the extremity of the Long Walk. The foreground here is formed of some noble beeches. Three miles farther south is

Virginia Water, one of the largest artificial lakes in England, surrounded by luxuriant foliage. At Old Windsor the windings of the river, with Ankerwyke in the foreground and Cooper's Hill behind, have long been favourite subjects with artists. Datchet on the opposite bank still retains some of the aspect of a country village. Langley Church is well worth a visit, if only to see the curious library attached to it. Upton Church, with its ivy-clad tower, contends with Stoke Poges for the honour of having inspired Gray. Slough is not a very lovely town, but here Herschel set up his great telescope; and a very pretty walk across fields from it takes us to Gray's Stoke Poges, and a longer walk to his Burnham Beeches. At Burnham itself is a village more primitive in appearance than any other I remember so near London. In the church are many monuments, among them one to a certain Wentworth who had to beg pardon of the House of Commons on his knees for proposing to inquire into Queen Elizabeth's civil list. A little farther south is Burnham Abbey, where he lived; and close to the Thames is Dorney, then, and still, the seat of the Palmers. On the right bank is St. Leonard's Hill, where more than one great statesman has

WINDSOR CASTLE FROM THE BROCAS.

resided, and whence one of the best views of the Castle may be obtained. A little farther off is Billingbear, once a seat of the Neviles; and beyond it again, Bray, whose Vicar has eclipsed the juster fame of the great architect who designed the roof of St. George's Chapel. Binfield is sacred to Alexander Pope, for there he wrote his early poem on Windsor Forest.

With such surroundings Windsor is the happiest hunting-ground of the English artist. Some there are who prefer grand scenery abroad to the lawns, and woods, and spires of our native land; but in all the world there is nothing so pleasing as 'English park-landscape,' as the Americans call it; and nowhere can it be studied to such advantage as here. It is not till we have travelled that we can fully appreciate its loveliness. The brown hills of Spain, even though the Sierra Nevada is behind them; the full, strong colours of the Mediterranean coast; the glassy coldness of the Alps; the warm pink and yellow of Egypt, to go no farther, do not give the same thrill of artistic delight. One tires of all other scenery, but not of this.

The Castle itself, artistically considered, is a little disappointing. Some of the old views by Sandby and by Hakewill, and others who drew at the beginning of the present century, show elements of picturesqueness which now only linger about the courts behind the Chapel. In the Upper Ward everything is spick and span; even the oldest buildings are re-faced. The Round Tower, which we would associate with Edward III. and the fair Lady Salisbury and the Order of the Garter, only dates, as we see it, from the time of George IV. Still, we must not be too exacting in this respect. The grand outline, as seen from a distance, is due to Wyatville; whatever there is of dignity in the composition is his work. The front towards the Long Walk has been criticised for its balance and symmetry; but it had always some such appearance, as we gather from the most ancient views. The great central feature, the Round Tower, was invisible from this side till Wyatville gave it its present proportions. Nevertheless, it must be allowed that the alterations he carried out went far to justify the epigram quoted by Mr. Thorne :—

> 'Let George, whose restlessness leaves nothing quiet,
> Change if he will the good old name of Wyatt:
> But let us hope that their united skill
> May not make Windsor Castle Wyatville.'

II.

Edward the Confessor at Old Windsor—Forged Deeds—The Grant to Westminster—William the Conqueror at New Windsor—The Norman Castle—Henry I.—The Constables—Wars of John—The Braoses—Magna Charta—Henry III.—His Buildings—His Treachery to the Citizens of London.

THAT Edward the Confessor resided at Old Windsor, at least occasionally, is certain from the dates of documents, and from the assertions of almost contemporary historians. One of the documents in question is a grant of land in Somerset to Gisa, bishop of Wells, and was signed and attested at 'Wendlesore.' The copy of the parchment is of later date, and, as is the case with an enormous mass of mediaeval charters, it may be a forgery. It occurs among the Cottonian manuscripts at the British Museum, and Kemble doubted its genuineness. Another document, of the authenticity of which there can be no doubt, is unfortunately without the year, though it was 'made at Windleshora on the fourth day of the Paschal Week,' and was witnessed by Queen Eadgitha, or

Edith, and by Earl Godwin and Earl Harold. In a third document mention is also made of Windsor. It is a long and pompous deed, of very questionable character, in which Edward is made to recapitulate many of the events of his reign, to refer to his projected visit to Rome, and to give, in satisfaction of his vow, a number of estates, one of them being Windsor, to the Abbey of Westminster. The date is December, 1065, the month before the King's death, the year before the conquest by the Normans. Fortunately, however, we have a shorter charter undated, in old English, easily turned into our modern language with the exception of a sentence or two, of the trustworthiness of which there can be no question. As an example it may be quoted whole, a few words only being altered :—

'Eadward Kynge greet all mine bishops, mine earls, mine thegns on Barrocscire [Berkshire] on Middlesex friendly : I kith [make known to] you that I have given Christ and St. Peter into Westmynstre Windlesoran and Stane [Staines] and all that thereto herth [belongs] within burh and without, with sac and with soc, with toll and with team, and with infangthief, on wood and on field, by strand and by land, on street and off street, and on all things so full and so forth as they stood with myself [as fully and as extensively as I myself held them], and I will not suffer that there any man any power shall have or any thing but the Abbot and monks for St. Peter's need. God you heal.'

Such are the terms of the grant, which resembles more the curt directness of some of the Conqueror's charters than the long-winded bombast in which the native English kings were wont on these occasions to indulge.

It was evidently towards the close of the reign of the Confessor that the grant was made; and the date of the larger deed, 'this fifth of the Kalends of January, 1066,' or, as we should say, 'the 28th December, 1065,' may very well be correct, as that was the day of the consecration of the great church at Westminster, the completion of which, far more than the good government of his kingdom, had been Edward's chief object in life. He was already so ill that he could not attend the ceremony, and he died on the 5th January.

It is not very easy to determine with any certainty the exact situation in Old Windsor of the house of King Edward. Yet the place is as little changed since his day as any place of the kind can be. The Thames still winds past the low, green meadows; the great trees still hang over the water;

the weir and the ferry and the fishing-ground remain where they were. The ninety houses of the Survey have partly disappeared, and there is now no well-defined village. It is impossible to imagine a sleepier little place. The road from the ferry winds through it between brick walls and palisades, and there is a perfume of flowers and of the leaves of aromatic shrubs. You come suddenly on the old, plain church, and remember that a church was on the spot—probably a wooden building—as early as the reign of the Confessor; and long before, no doubt. Near the church may be traced the moat of Tile Place Farm. It is not quadrangular, nor is it very large, nor is it, again, even traditionally, the Manor House; yet here, according to many authorities, was the 'palace' of Edward the Confessor.

In fine weather Old Windsor is a pleasant and quiet nook, surrounded by the scenes of all kinds of great events, yet itself without anything, except its own simple beauty, to excite the interest of the traveller. One of the daughters of George III. made herself a residence here, at first a mere tea-cottage, afterwards a house; but there are very few monuments of interest in the church, and what is left of the village consists chiefly of small isolated houses, with pretty gardens and tall trees. The parish is very small, but there is, or was, an out-

OLD WINDSOR CHURCH.

lying district beyond the Great Park. So utterly has the original Windsor been eclipsed by the half hide on the hill above it, in the parish of Clewer, upon which William built his castle, that after this point in history Windsor means the Castle of the Conqueror and the town which grew up at its foot. Yet William must certainly for a short time have made it his residence, and it is not always possible to decide whether charters and writs were dated from the Old or the New Windsor. William took Old Windsor into his own hands from the first, on account of 'the pleasantness of the situation,' as he says, and compensated the Abbot and monks of Westminster by the gift of two manors in Essex and certain other lands. Exchanges to which a king of England was one of the parties—as in this case, and as in the case of Hyde Park and its appurtenances in the reign of Henry VIII.—were not unfrequently of a somewhat one-sided character.

'On the day King Edward was alive and dead,' as the usual formula in the Domesday Book expresses it, then, Old Windsor was owned by the monks of the newly finished Abbey of Westminster, and the neighbouring Manor of Clewer was the estate of the new King Harold. As Harold had been earl of that part of the kingdom which lay south of the Thames from beyond Oxford to Chertsey, the stronghold on the chalk hill in the great bend of the river must have been a conveniently situated place of residence, the more so on account of its nearness to the occasional dwelling of King Edward at Old Windsor. But it was probably the forest which determined William of Normandy in his choice of it for one of his castles. There is less mention of New Windsor in the chronicles of the time than of many other fortresses not so important in later years. We do not know when William first began to build on the Saxon earthworks. Several of his charters and other acts are dated at Windsor; but we have no means of making sure which Windsor is meant until we come to the line as to the Castle, quoted from the Domesday Survey in our last chapter.

From that time there is no doubt. Norman remains, pointing to the existence of very extensive buildings on the south side of the Upper Ward, lead to the supposition that the quadrangle was completed, counting the mound as its western side. No Norman remains have been identified with certainty in the Lower Ward, the oldest buildings only going back to the time of Henry III. Strange to say, it is impossible to find out what building, if any, William placed upon the mound. As it is 125 feet in diameter, there would be room for a considerable tower; but no record of such a tower exists, and it is possible, and not altogether contrary to analogy, that nothing stronger than the Saxon palisade crowned it before the time of Henry III. Its height of 70 feet above the ditch would be a great element of strength in itself. There would, moreover, be nothing unusual in postponing the erection of a stone keep on the mound. Mr. Clark ('Mediaeval Military Architecture,' 42) is clear on the point, though he does not name Windsor as an example. The Normans, he says, where the site was old, and there was a mound, as at Lincoln, Huntingdon, Rockingham, Wallingford, or York, 'seem to have been content to repair the existing works, usually of timber only, and to have postponed the replacing of them with a regular shell till a more convenient season, which in many cases did not occur for a century.' If any timber fortress in England was likely to be strong and well built, it would be at Clewer, where wood was plenty, and where so martial an earl as Harold was lord of the manor. Certain it is, that even in the reign of Edward III. no building of importance stood on the mound until he founded the Order of the Garter, and very few Norman remains were found when Wyatville dug into the chalk, and they were of a late type. Yet, whatever may have been the character of the fortification on the summit of the mound, there is now no doubt that the earliest builders of Windsor Castle chose not the Lower, but the Upper Ward, for their principal works; and although nothing remains above ground of the Castle as it stood before the reign of Henry III., traces have been found in recent years of subterraneous passages, with distinct features of Norman architecture, beneath the modern building on the southern and eastern sides of what are now the private apartments of the Sovereign. One of these, very nearly under the private entrance of the Castle, consists of a passage in the chalk which formerly constituted a secret outlet towards the ditch. Such passages are, of course, not generally accessible, and the ditch itself has been obliterated, at least on that side; and as there are in numberless places, wherever a house of ancient date still stands, traditions of secret entrances and secret exits, the existence of one which is not only real and still extant, and which moreover leads through the royal residence itself, is well worth noting.

William Rufus assembled a council at Windsor

in 1095, and there imprisoned Mowbray when he had taken him in the north. It is impossible to say in what part of the Castle Mowbray lived out the remaining thirty years of his life; but the King held his Christmas the next year at the Castle, and William, bishop of Durham, died there during the week's festivities. The King was back at Easter and Whitsuntide in the following year, and thence made his march into Wales. Henry I. also constantly visited Windsor, and is said by several authorities to have built the town, and to have greatly enlarged and improved the Castle. Henry also built a chapel, which he dedicated to Edward the Confessor, providing it with five priests, but without endowments, the priests being paid out of the Exchequer. This chapel in all probability stood on the site now covered by the Albert Memorial Chapel, formerly known as Wolsey's Tomb-house; and it must have been here that, in 1121, Henry married his second wife, Adelicia of Louvain, the 'Fair Maid of Brabant.' Henry must have been but a melancholy husband, if it is true that he never smiled after his son was drowned. He had been a widower for two years. The wedding was the cause of a singular dispute. Windsor at that time was in the diocese of Salisbury, and Roger le Poor, then its bishop, was not the man to renounce any privilege which he possessed, or thought he possessed. He claimed the right to perform the marriage, but the council decided that Ralph, the archbishop of Canterbury, should officiate.

A similar contest took place during the Christmas festival in 1127. Henry received at Windsor the homage of all the great officials, both clergy and laity, whom he caused to swear allegiance to his daughter and heiress, the Empress Maud. As was usual on such occasions the coronation ceremony was repeated, and Thurstan, archbishop of York, thought himself entitled to officiate, to the prejudice of William de Corboyl, the archbishop of Canterbury. He was, however, prevented, 'and his cross-bearer, who had carried his cross into the king's chapel, was turned out, together with the cross he was carrying.'

The office of Constable of Windsor had been granted by the Conqueror to Walter Fitz-Other, the lord of the manor of Eton, on the opposite side of the Thames. His family assumed the surname of Windsor, and several of them seem to have enjoyed the office; but when, in 1153, the treaty of

Wallingford confirmed the peace between Henry, afterwards Henry II., and King Stephen, Windsor was delivered to the custody of Richard de Lucy. The mention of the fortress in Stephen's charter is peculiar. It is called *Mota* de Windsor. It would perhaps be going too far to assume that this means that the mound was not covered by a keep, but it increases the probability which I have already mentioned ; and which is further strengthened by the fact that the Castle does not figure at all in the annals of Stephen's wars. It seems to have been a favourite residence of Henry II., and in his tenth year we read of the expenditure of 30*s*. on the kitchen. Henry here received the Irish ambassadors of Roderick, king of Connaught, and, 1185, he here knighted his son John previous to sending him on his expedition into Ireland. One of the chroniclers tells a sad tale connected with Henry's works at Windsor. 'It is recorded,' says Fabyan, 'that in a chambere at Wyndsore he caused to be painted an eagle, with four birds, whereof three of them all rased [scratched] the body of the old eagle, and the fourth was scratching at the old eagle's eyes. When the question was asked of him what thing that picture should signify? it was answered by him, "This old eagle," said he, "is myself; and these four eagles betoken my four sons, the

THE CLOISTERS AND THE DEANERY.

which cease not to pursue my death, and especially my youngest son John, which now I love most, shall most especially await and imagine my death."¹

John himself was destined to suffer much at Windsor. His father had left the buildings in good repair, and, during the absence on the Crusade of Richard I., it was handed over to the keeping of Bishop Pudsey of Durham, while the Tower of London was given similarly to his rival Longchamps, bishop of Ely, who was Chancellor; but Pudsey was no match for Longchamps, who soon obtained possession of the Castle; and, even after he had been once deprived of it, he took it again, and it was from Windsor that he made the memorable flight to the Tower which led to his temporary deposition. The Castle was placed in the custody of Walter, archbishop of Rouen. Walter was dispossessed of it by John, when he returned from France in 1193, but took it again after a short siege, and put some of its defenders to death, John retiring again to France. When he became King he was frequently here. In 1205 he writes hence to Reginald de Cornhill, an eminent London merchant, to send him two small casks of wine, and a book called the Romance of the History of England ('Romantium de Historia Anglorum'). It would be impossible, without unduly prolonging the notice of this reign, to detail all John's doings at Windsor; but two transactions cannot be passed over. According to some of the chroniclers it was here and not at Corfe that the King starved Maud de Braose and her son to death. There are great discrepancies in the story, which, though it is told by many different historians, may be entirely false, although no one doubts that John, who certainly imprisoned some members of the Braose family at Windsor, was quite capable of such a crime. The second event of this reign with which Windsor is prominently connected is the granting of Magna Charta.

Between Old Windsor and Staines, on the London Road, but within the boundaries of Surrey, is the flat meadow of Runimede. The towers of the Castle are visible from it, and John, during the conferences which preceded and followed the ratification of the charter, went backwards and forwards each day. The charter is dated, '*in prato quod vocatur Runimed*,' on the 15th June, but was probably not signed before the 23rd, when the conference terminated. It has been asserted that the word Runimede signifies 'Council Meadow,' which would point to some previous meeting of the same kind there; and Edward the Confessor is said to have met his Witanagemot at the spot. But these stories, like the identification of Magna Charta Island, are either conjecture or local tradition and very unsafe foundations for history. After the conference John remained three days longer at Windsor, whence he departed to Odiham. He was back at Windsor when he heard of the landing of Louis in 1216, and this was his last visit.

One turns with relief from the reign of John; but Henry III. made Windsor the scene of as shocking a piece of treachery as any ever perpetrated by his father.

When he had been five years on the throne and had reached the mature age of fifteen, he began to turn his attention to the repair of the Castle. Vast sums were spent in a few years, both here and at Westminster, on buildings. The old hall, which was among the Norman buildings in the Upper Ward, was abandoned for a new and larger one which stood in the Lower Ward, near the north-western corner of the cliff. It has been identified, in part, with the library of the Dean and Chapter, and the rest of Henry's domestic buildings seem to have been close by. Henry IV., when the 'King's house' was once more in the Upper Ward, granted the site for canons' residences, and the charmingly irregular and picturesque row of dwellings of various dates which lies north of the nave of St. George's Chapel, contains many relics of the time of Henry III. In 1272 he roofed the Keep, and, for aught we know to the contrary, he may have been the first to place a stone tower on the mound. His tower cannot, however, have been of a very substantial character, as Edward III. found no building on the mound suitable for the celebrations of the new Order of St. George. If Edward's own building, the Round Tower, was an improvement on its predecessor, Henry III. cannot have constructed anything of much importance, for until Wyatville raised it to its present height it was by no means worthy of its lofty and conspicuous situation.

Instead of going minutely through the progress of Henry's works at Windsor, it will be best briefly to describe the probable appearance of the Castle when he first took it in hand, and again at the conclusion of his reign. The buildings as they stood when he inherited their possession had probably very slight and meagre defences on the west side towards the town. The outer ditch was shallow, and of towers along the wall we know nothing. It was, in fact, merely the first defence of what was literally the outer court. A second ditch seems to have been drawn across the court, and I understand that Mr. Clark is inclined to think that the Horse Shoe Cloister marks an inner ring of the ancient earthworks. There was a deep ditch round the mound, and possibly the present so-called Norman Gate marks the principal entrance to the better fortified portion of the Castle. It was approached, no doubt, by a bridge and portcullis. Another gate stood on the south side, very near the modern George the Fourth's Gateway. It also was approached over the great ditch of the Castle by a bridge, and a third bridge is mentioned in early records. The eastern side of the upper quadrangle, as well as the northern and southern, probably contained apartments protected by towers. What is now a sunk garden and the eastern terrace was then a steeply-scarped cliff of chalk. The great hall of the Castle was in the Upper Ward, and the chamber used by the King's eldest son must have been on the north side. All these buildings, and whatever stood upon the mound, were at this time very much dilapidated. Except a small chapel we cannot speak with certainty of any buildings in the Lower Ward.

When Henry had completed his alterations the

THE NORMAN GATEWAY.

old walls of the Upper Ward were renewed and crenellated, and the chief residence of the King

THE NORMAN GATE.

transferred to the Lower Ward, which was divided longitudinally into two parts, the place of the present

St. George's Chapel being occupied by the western end of a smaller chapel. The new great hall, the kitchen, and other domestic buildings, were connected with the Bell Tower at the north-west corner at one end, and with 'a certain apartment for the King's use,' which must have looked down over the steep cliff, where are now the Hundred Steps. Beside it, and under the same roof, were the Queen's apartments, and between them and the chapel there was a grass-plot. The chapel had a porch, a cloister, and a bell-tower. Part of the cloister still stands as it was then, and a portrait of the King, part of the painted decoration, was not long ago discovered and glazed over. This wall-painting, although it is unquestionably not unlike the King's portrait on his tomb at Westminster, may be the face of a sacred personage, other than the King, forming part of a large composition. It is within the arcade of Henry's work on the northern face of the old wall of what is now the Memorial Chapel. Another fragment is by the chapel door.

On the town side of the Castle three great towers were built, and a postern made beneath them. On the north side, near the Keep, was a new tower, on the same site as that now known as the Winchester Tower. A gateway was probably constructed at the same time, at or near the place now occupied by the Gateway of Henry VIII. The

THE HUNDRED STEPS.

fortifications on the south side of the Lower Ward were completed by a tower still known by the name of Henry III. All these buildings were handsomely decorated with painting and the windows filled with glass. In the latter years of Henry's reign some improvements were made in the Upper Ward, where new rooms were built for the Queen, with an oratory and private chapel.

In one of the new towers on the western side was possibly the dungeon, which Henry used for the imprisonment of the Londoners after the death of Earl Simon. Henry had a terrible quarrel with the citizens. They had long resisted his exactions, and among their number there was none who had carried himself so bravely towards the tyrant as Fitz-Thomas, the Mayor. When, in 1265, the King had been in a kind of semi-captivity in London, while Simon di Montfort governed the kingdom in his name, Fitz-Thomas had addressed to him in St. Paul's words which Henry took as a personal insult. When the battle of Evesham set him free to wreak his vengeance, he summoned the Mayor and the principal citizens to Windsor, giving them a safe-conduct. They set out on Friday, the 5th of October, 1265, to the number of forty, and reached Windsor in a couple of days. The King sent messengers to say that he was not ready for them, but that they were to enter the Castle, and that on the morrow they should learn his will. Upon this they entered, and were immediately taken to the Keep

as prisoners, 'the letters of safe-conduct from the King availing them nought.' There they remained throughout that night and the next day. In the evening the greater number of them were allowed to descend into the Lower Ward, where they were lodged; but the Mayor and four of his companions were detained in the custody of 'Sir Edward le Fitz-Roy,' afterwards King Edward I. From this imprisonment it does not seem that Fitz-Thomas ever emerged; the others were eventually released, but his name does not occur in the list of those pardoned some years later; and whether he died in the dungeons of the Clewer Tower or lived out a long imprisonment in the Keep on the mound, we have no further information about him. The King went to London and confiscated the houses and property of his principal enemies, and though the people clamoured for the Mayor of their choice they never beheld him again. That Henry, in spite of the magnificence of his buildings and the purity of his taste in art, was a worthy son of his father, King John, could be proved from this treacherous act alone.

III.

A Tournament—Birth of Edward III.—Renovation of the Castle—The Round Tower and the Round Table—Royal Prisoners—The Founders of the Order of the Garter—The Death of Philippa—Richard II. at Windsor—His Farewell to Queen Isabel—Plot at Windsor against Henry IV.—James of Scotland—The Heart of St. George—Birth of Henry VI.—Edward IV.—His Body Examined—Visit of the King of Castile—Henry VIII.—The Earl of Surrey—Burial-place of Henry VIII. and Queen Jane Seymour.

THE glories of the reign of Edward III. are connected more intimately with Windsor Castle than with any other place. Edward I., although his beautiful queen, Eleanor, seems to have resided much in the Castle, only visited it occasionally, and never kept a Christmas here. His two eldest sons were born at Windsor while Henry III. was still living, and they and their brother, Alphonso, all seem to have died here. Prince Alphonso had reached the mature age of ten, and a marriage with a Spanish princess had been arranged for him. A Psalter illuminated with his arms and those of his intended bride is in the British Museum, and is interesting as giving us some early examples of heraldic bearings. In the Record Office there is a roll describing the purchases made in preparation for a tournament at Windsor in July, 1278, when the boy was only five; and among the payments is one of fifteen shillings for his shield, and another of forty pounds for his dress of coloured cloth, which may mean something of the nature of a tabard.

This tournament is described as taking place in the Park, which probably means the Little Park, below the Castle, now traversed diagonally by the road to Datchet. The knights were dressed in leather armour, gilt or silvered, according to their rank, and wore crests also of leather, their swords being blunted so as to avoid injury. This is an early mention of crests, and whether they were figures of heraldic animals in *cuir boulli*, coloured and gilt, or were repetitions of the coat-of-arms, as in the nearly contemporary Louterell Psalter, I cannot say.

Edward II. was more often at Windsor than his father, but the events of his reign do not greatly connect him with the place, except during 1312. In that year, on the 23rd November, at forty minutes past five in the morning, 'the 6 degree of the sign Scorpio ascending, and the 18 degree of Leo culminating,' the young Queen Isabella, then only eighteen years of age, gave birth here to the prince who was destined to do so much for Windsor Castle. He was born on Monday and baptized on the following Thursday in the old chapel of St. Edward, being called after his father, and grandfather, and the royal saint, and having three bishops and four other great men as his godfathers.

He succeeded to the throne on the deposition of his unfortunate father in January, 1326, and from that time to the end of his long reign Windsor was the almost constant scene of tournaments, processions, feasts, chapters, and assemblies, in which everything was subordinated to pomp and display. This is not the place to detail the history of the wars with France and Scotland, except in so far as they concern Windsor; but here, we know, the royal and noble prisoners were conducted after each triumph, and here Edward celebrated each victory in the enlarged chapel. The old 'Aula Regis,' the King's palace in which he had been born, was given up to be the residence of the canons of a new ecclesiastical foundation, and St. George was associated with St.

Edward the Confessor as the patron saint. At first a 'Warden,' or 'Custos,' presided over the Chapter, but in the last year of the reign of Henry IV. his title was changed to 'Dean.' Besides canons and vicars there were appointed twenty-six 'alms-knights,' an institution out of which has grown the modern band of pensioners known as the Military and Naval Knights. The first 'Poor Knights' were nominated by the first knights of the new Order of the Garter, each choosing one valiant soldier who in his old age had fallen on evil days, and was weak in body, indigent, and decayed.

Before we come to the first chapter of the Order we must see what preparations Edward made for the reception of the knights companions. The Upper Ward was almost rebuilt, and under the State apartments built in the time of Charles II., and refaced by Wyatville, are still to be seen the vaulted chambers of Edward's basement. The great Bishop, William of Wykeham, was the architect, and from him the Winchester Tower obtained its name. It is said that the motto, '*Hoc Fecit Wykeham*,' was placed upon it, and that the wily prelate interpreted it to the King as meaning not 'Wykeham made this,' but 'This made Wykeham.'

THE LOWER WARD.

This tradition is probably no more true than another one to the effect that the Kings of France and Scotland, while prisoners, when walking with King Edward in the Lower Ward, pointed out that

INTERIOR OF THE GREAT HALL.

the Upper Ward lay on higher ground, and commanded a finer view, and that the King 'approved their sayings, adding pleasantly that it should so be, and that he would bring his castle thither, that is to say, enlarge it so far with two other wards, the charges whereof should be borne with their two ransoms.' Stow, who tells this story, adds, ' as after it came to pass ;' but though it is possible enough that the not very refined manners of the age permitted King Edward to talk and even to joke with his captives as to their ransoms, it is certain, as we have seen, that the Upper Ward was in existence long before, and that Edward's greatest works in that part of the Castle had been in progress for many years before either King John or King David came hither as prisoners.

It is asserted on better grounds that some time in the beginning of his reign Edward with his Queen visited Glastonbury, where the Abbot showed them the tomb of King Arthur, and, opening it, displayed the gigantic bones of the legendary king. Although Froissart may be in error in making 1344 the date of the institution of the Garter, it is certain that the story of King Arthur and his Round Table had already obtained universal credence, and the addition to it which made his knights assemble at Windsor was willingly received. 'At this time Edward, king of England, resolved,' says Froissart, 'to rebuild the great castle of Windsor, formerly built and founded by King Arthur, and where was first set up and established the noble Round Table, from whence so many valiant men and knights have issued forth to perform feats of arms and

A SKETCH IN THE STEWARD'S ROOM.

prowess throughout the world.' We need not take up our space by recapitulating the arguments for and against Froissart's date, but it is more than probable that the idea of a brotherhood of this kind gradually grew up, and that by 1348 it had taken complete shape. Through all the country proclamations were made summoning builders, and carpenters, and other workmen, to complete the building. The old tower on the mound was removed, whatever it may have been, and the Round Tower was constructed for the Round Table. It was built in haste, of chalk faced with better stone from Wheatley, 'which the Dean of St. Paul's had collected for his own building operations, but was persuaded to give up to the King, and three shiploads brought direct from Caen.' The table itself was set round the courtyard, and seems, from what can be made out, to have been in the shape rather of a horseshoe than of a full circle, so that the attendants could stand in the middle to serve the guests. Fifty-two oaks were brought from Reading to Westminster, where the King's workmen made the table, and forwarded it to the Castle.

Here assembled the founders of this famous Order, and we can picture them as they filed in, each knight wearing over his armour the long surcoat embroidered with his arms. His helmet has a visor, which, when seen in profile, looks like the beak of a bird, but it is probably carried by his

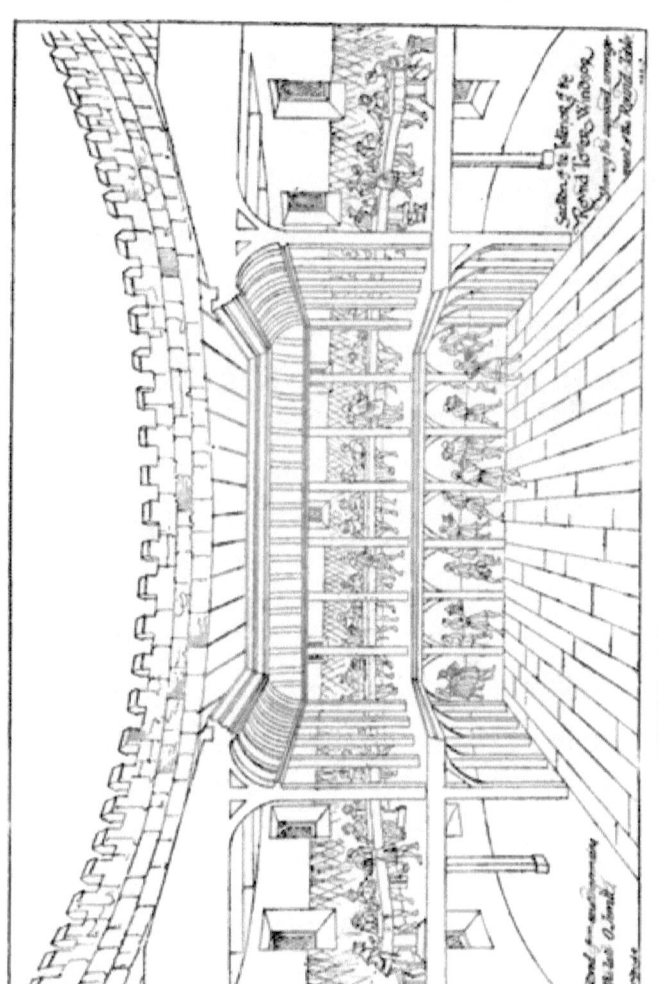

SECTION OF THE INTERIOR OF THE ROUND TOWER.

Colonel Maude, V.C., Military Knight of Windsor, died suddenly on Friday night at Windsor Castle, aged 72. He was the eldest son of the late Hon. Captain F. Maude, R.N. He joined the Royal Artillery in 1847, and commanded the guns of Havelock's column in his march to Cawnpore. Afterwards he took part in the repeated attempts to relieve the Lucknow garrison, which, it will be remembered, was partly effected on September 25th, 1857. Colonel Maude later assisted at the capture in the following year. Three times he was recommended for the Victoria Cross, once by the unanimous (ballot) vote of the men of his battery, and he at length gained it for his conduct in leading the force on the road from Alumbagh to the Canal Bridge, Lucknow, September 25th, 1857, where one-third of his men were killed or wounded during thirty minutes' fighting. He was the author of one or two publications dealing with military matters.

THE LATE MARQUIS OF BUTE.

HEART TO BE INTERRED IN PALESTINE.

The Marchioness of Bute, Lady Margaret Stuart, her daughter, and Lord Colum Edmund, her son, left Mount Stuart on Saturday for London, en route to Palestine. They have with them the heart of the late Marquis, for burial at Mount Olivet—a condition made in his will. The heart of King Robert the Bruce, an ancestor of the late Marquis, was carried by the "Black Douglas" for interment in the Holy Land. But the Douglas was slain fighting with the Moors in Spain, and the casket with the Royal heart was brought back to Scotland, and buried in Melrose Abbey.

squire, and he wears upon his head a bonnet of velvet or silk, perhaps also embroidered with his

THE KITCHEN COURT, WINDSOR CASTLE.

arms. His armour consists chiefly of ring-mail, but breast-plates and back-pieces were coming into use, and gauntlets, as well as the defences of the arms and legs, were frequently of plate.

Besides the warlike King himself and his heroic son, the Black Prince, there assembled among the other twenty-four founders many of the heroes of Froissart's delightful pages. There was Warwick, who made prisoner the Archbishop of Seinz at the battle of Poitiers, and afterwards obtained the enormous sum of 8000*l.* for his ransom, and who, when he died of the plague in 1369, left 'not behind him his equal.' There was the young Earl of Salisbury, whose beautiful mother has so often, in a story of the sixteenth century, been said to have given rise to the motto of the Garter. There was Thomas, Earl of Kent in right of his wife, the 'Fair Maid,' who afterwards married the Black Prince. There was Sir Neile Loring, who had contributed so largely to the great naval victory at Sluys. There was Sir James Audley, who was so badly wounded at Poitiers, where he had made the first assault. There was Sir Sanchet D'Abrichecourt, whose father and mother had succoured Queen Isabella and her son when Edward II. drove them into Flanders. There was Chandos, who twice took prisoner the French champion, Du Guesclin. There was the young Mortimer, to whom the King had restored the lands and titles of his grandfather. But we cannot go through the whole list, nor can we even mention those who came after. Before Edward's long reign was ended the stalls had been occupied by sixty-three knights, the last admitted being Henry, Earl of Derby, who afterwards became himself, as King Henry IV., Sovereign of the Order.

Windsor was the scene of the last parting of Edward and Philippa, so touchingly described by Froissart. It was on the 'Vigil of the Assumption,' 15 August, 1369, and

'there fell in England a heavy case and a common, howbeit it was right piteous for the King, his children, and all his realm. For the good Queen of England, that so many good deeds had done in her time, and so many knights succoured, and ladies and damsels comforted, and had so largely departed of her goods to her people, and naturally loved always the nation of Hainault, the country where she was born; she fell sick in the castle of Windsor, the which sickness continued on her so long that there was no remedy but death. And the good lady, when she knew and perceived that there was with her no remedy but death, she desired to speak with the King, her husband. And when he was before her she put out of her bed her right hand, and took the King by his right hand, who was right sorrowful at his heart. Then she said, "Sir, we have in peace, joy, and great prosperity used all our time together. Sir, now I pray you, at our departing, that ye will grant me three desires." The King, right sorrowfully weeping, said, "Madam, desire what ye will, I grant it." "Sir," said she, "I require you, first of all, that all manner of people such as I have dealt withal in their merchandise, on this side the sea or beyond, that it may please you to pay everything that I owe to them or to any other. And secondly, sir, all such ordinances and promises as I have made to the churches as well of this country as beyond the sea, whereas I have had my devotion, that it may please you to accomplish and fulfil the same. Thirdly, sir, I require you that it may please you to take none other sepulture when so ever it shall please God to call you out of this transitory life but beside me in Westminster." The King, all weeping, said, "Madam, I grant all your desire." Then the good lady and Queen made on her the sign of the cross, and recommended the King, her husband, to God, and her youngest son, Thomas, who was beside her. And anon after, she yielded up the spirit, the which I believe surely the holy angels received with great joy up to heaven, for in all her life she did neither in thought nor deed thing whereby to lese her soul, as far as any creature could know.'

With the death of Philippa Edward's good fortune seemed to desert him. They had been married more than forty years, and their eldest son, the Black Prince, was now thirty-nine. In the following year he was invalided home from the army in France, and never served again. But there is little to connect the melancholy remainder of this reign with Windsor.

Some of the most important scenes of the life of Richard II. are laid in Windsor Castle. Here, in 1386, while he was celebrating St. George's Day with the usual pomp, the deputation of London citizens waited on him and insisted on being heard as to their grievances. Here he imprisoned Suffolk, releasing him, however, as soon as Parliament was dissolved. In 1390 he appointed Geoffrey Chaucer the poet to superintend the repairs of the chapel. A second time, in 1391, the Londoners came to Windsor to remonstrate with the King, and he appears to have held two ex-mayors in custody here at the same time. The great dispute between Henry, Duke of Hereford, who, as I have said, was the last Knight of the Garter admitted by his grandfather, Edward III., and the Duke of Norfolk, took place at Windsor, where, in the courtyard of the Castle, King Richard sat upon a platform with his bishops and lords about him, and called before him the two dukes. Shakespeare erroneously places the scene in London, but the Duke of Norfolk was at that time actually in the custody of the Governor of Windsor Castle, and had obtained leave to summon armourers from London to make his coat-of-mail for the intended combat.

Richard bid a last farewell to his child-queen Isabella of France, on the 25th of April, 1399. She was only eleven years of age at this time. The scene is affectingly described in a contemporary chronicle, which tells us how Richard and Isabel walked hand in hand from the Castle to the Lower Court, and entered the Deanery, passing thence into the chapel.

'The canons chaunted very sweetly, and the King himself chaunted a collect, and afterwards made his offering. He then took the Queen in his arms and kissed her twelve or thirteen times, saying sorrowfully, "Adieu, *ma chère*, until we meet again; I commend me to you." Thus spoke the King in the presence of all the people, and the Queen began to weep, saying to the King, "Alas! my lord, will you leave me here?"'

We are then told how the King and Queen partook of wine and comfits at the Deanery, and how he again kissed her many times, lifting her in his arms.

'And by our Lady, I never saw so great a lord make so much of nor show such great affection to a lady as did King Richard to his Queen. Great pity was it that they separated, for never saw they each other more.'

After Richard's death Isabella was detained some time by Henry IV., who would have married her to his eldest son. Eventually she married the Duke of Orleans, reversing her own position with Richard II., for she was much older than her second husband.

One of the numerous conspiracies against Henry IV. came to a head at Windsor, when the Duke of Exeter and others seized and searched the Castle, hoping to find and kill the King; 'but, as it fortuned, the King had warning, and anon he rode to London and made him strong to ride on his adversaries aforesaid.' Among those concerned in this abortive rebellion was the unfortunate Sir Bernard Brocas, who was shortly afterwards beheaded in London. During the whole of Henry's reign the young Earl of March was kept a prisoner in the Castle. He was of course the senior male heir of Edward III., and his descendants subsequently ascended the throne in the person of Edward IV. Here he had a companion in misfortune in James Stewart, the young King of Scotland, who, after being some time in the Tower of London, was brought to Windsor in 1413. He was lodged in the tower immediately south-east of the Mound, from the top of which he saw and fell in love with Joanna Beaufort, the King's niece, whom he eventually married. The scene of his famous poem, 'The King's Quair,' is laid at Windsor. He had much liberty during his nominal captivity, and attended the coronation of Queen Katherine, afterwards serving for a short time under Henry V. in France. This was probably the happiest time of his life. His return to Scotland was marked by the execution of his nearest relatives, and he was himself assassinated in 1437.

The prisoners of Agincourt were also detained at Windsor. In 1416 the feast of St. George was deferred until May in order that the Emperor Sigismund might be present at it. He brought as an offering the heart of St. George, which remained in the chapel till the Reformation.

A curious anecdote is concerned with the birth of Henry, Prince of Wales, afterwards Henry VI. It is related by three of the chroniclers that as the King was besieging Meaux he received the news of his son's birth.

'But when he heard reported the places of his nativity, were it that he, warned by some prophesie, or had some fore-knowledge, or else judged himself of his son's fortune, he said unto the Lord Fitz Hugh, his trusty chamberlain, these words, "My lord, I, Henry, born at Monmouth, shall small time reign and much get, and Henry, born at Windsor, shall long reign and all lose: but as God will so be it."'

Henry of Windsor spent all his early years at his birthplace. The fabric of the Castle was much neglected, and the lands about were let out to farm. On his marriage with Margaret of Anjou some necessary repairs were made, and during the King's illness in 1453 he lived here. Of his great foundation at Eton we shall speak in a later chapter. Edward IV. was the first king buried at Windsor, where his little daughter, Mary, and his son, George, had been buried before him. He desired in his last will that over his sepulchre there should be made a vault of convenient height, and over it a chapel with a tomb, on which was to be his figure in silver, and 'about the same tomb scripture made convenient, remembering the day and year of our decease.' But all that was ever carried out of these directions was the placing of a curious screen of elaborate ironwork at the north side of the choir. About a hundred years ago George III. directed the name of Edward IV. to be cut on a tablet in the north aisle. In 1492 Elizabeth Wydeville was buried beside her husband by direction of Henry VII., and a curious account exists of the funeral, which was celebrated without pomp 'or costlie expenses doune thereabought.'

In 1484 the body of Henry VI., who had been buried at Chertsey Abbey, was removed to Windsor and buried on the opposite side of the choir from Edward IV. under a monument of which nothing remains. In 1789 both his grave and that of his rival were opened by workmen. The coffin of Edward IV. was examined only:—

'It was of lead, seven feet long, and was much compressed in some parts, and a little decayed. On opening it the entire skeleton was found, measuring six feet, three inches and a half in length. Some brown hair was found lying near the skull and neck. The coffin also contained a liquid, which at the feet was three inches deep, and which Dr. Lind, who examined it, pronounced to be the result of the decomposition of the body.'

The remains appear to have been treated with very scant respect. A lock of the hair is in the Ashmolean Museum at Oxford, and a bone of the leg was publicly sold with the museum of a private collector by auction in London a few years ago.

It was understood at the time that the dishonoured relic was taken back to Windsor and restored to its proper place.

The great work carried on by Edward IV. and Henry VII. which made the chapel what it now is, must be noticed separately in a subsequent chapter.

Philip, king of Castille, visited Henry VII. at Windsor in 1506, when there were great solemnities, all of which are fully chronicled in a paper among the Cottonian MSS. From it we learn 'that his Grace rode towards the said King of Castille a mile or more out of Windsor, and there, in an arable field, met with him;' and that when the King of Castille 'perceived the King he took off his hat, and in like manner the King took off his, and with a loving and glad countenance each saluted and embraced other.'

When they reached the Castle they went through the royal apartments, which are described for us. First there was the Nether Gallery, next they went up the stairs, and then through the Upper Gallery to the King's great chamber, which was richly hung with arras, and contained 'a rich bed.' Here the knights and esquires remained, and the barons and bannerets attended the two kings to the next chamber, and from thence to a third, 'which was hanged with a very rich arras, in the which there was a cloth of estate and as rich a bed as I have seen.' Here the bishops and earls stopped, and there was a contest of politeness between the two kings as to entering the last chamber. For the 'King of Castille excused him, and said that the King should not take the pains to convey him to his lodgings.' Eventually, 'for any words or thing the King could do, he would convey the King to his lodgings, and so he did,' that is, he accompanied Henry; and the King 'would have somewhat reconveyed him, but the King of Castille would not suffer it.' Of the Park we read that on the third of February 'both Kings heard mass in their own closets, and after dinner went a hunting in the Little Park, where every each of the Kings killed certain deer, their own hands, with their own crossbows.'

We also read of a new tower, from which King Philip witnessed the baiting of a horse, and of a tennis-court which seems to have stood on the western side of the Upper Ward, close under the Round Tower. Philip was admitted a Knight of the Garter, and the writer speaks of a great cup-

HENRY VIII.'S GATE.

board which 'continually stood in the great hall with all gilt plate.'

Henry VIII., in the first year of his reign, built the gateway which still bears his name in the Lower Ward, but this appears to be the only improvement he made, although the works in the chapel were continued for several years. The poet Earl of Surrey was much at Windsor in his early life, and was a prisoner there about the year 1546. In one of his poems he gives a description of the large green courts, the stately seats, the secret groves, the wild forest, and other delights of the place. He was not long confined on that occasion, but on the 12th of December of the same year he was again arrested, and early in 1547 was beheaded, a few days only before the death of the King, whose last formal act was to appoint a commission to give the royal assent to the bill of attainder against the Earl and the Duke of Norfolk, his father.

Another victim of Henry's tyranny flits across the stage at Windsor for a moment. This was Anne Boleyn, who was here created Marchioness of Pembroke with great solemnity in 1532. We are not told the reasons which led to the burial of Queen Jane Seymour at Windsor after her death at Hampton Court in 1537. Her funeral was conducted with great pomp, a life-sized figure of the deceased being upon the pall, with a rich crown of gold upon the head, the hair all loose, a sceptre of gold in the right hand, and adorned with finger-rings and a necklace of gold and precious stones.

The long tragedy of the closing years of Henry's life was enacted rather at the Tower of London than at Windsor Castle. Why he should have chosen Windsor for his tomb we do not know, except that Queen Jane had been laid in St. George's Chapel. At the time of her death he showed for once in his life genuine grief, and retired, we are told, to a solitary place, not to be spoken with. His councillors 'took order' about the funeral, so that it is possibly owing to them that neither she nor Henry rests in the gorgeous mausoleum at Westminster erected by Henry VII. The tomb at Windsor was never completed, though the King left elaborate directions about it in his will, together with sums of money to the Dean and Chapter, to the Poor Knights, and others, entreating them to pray for his soul, and appointing regular masses to be said for his repose. After an appeal to the Blessed Virgin and all the company of heaven to pray for him, he goes on to direct that his body and that of his 'true and loving wife, Queen Jane,' should be buried in the same place, and that an honourable tomb, with a fair grate about it, should be provided. This was never done, though Stow says he saw the railings in copper cast, but they were probably destroyed at the same time as the bronze ornaments of Wolsey's sarcophagus, under the Commonwealth. So completely was the place left unmarked that when, ninety-eight years later, they sought a grave for the body of Charles I., it 'was a fellow of the town who undertook to tell them' where was the vault which contained the remains of Henry VIII. and Jane Seymour. According to another account it was one of the aged Poor Knights who found the spot; and, according to a third, it was found by trying the pavement 'to see if a sound would confess any hollowness therein.' The vault was once more opened for the interment of a child of Queen Anne; and again in 1813, when the Prince Regent was present at an examination of the body of Charles. On that occasion the great coffin of Henry and the small one of his queen by its side were seen for the last time.

IV.

Early Views of the Castle — Queen Elizabeth's *Boethius* — Norden's View — The Dragon's Fountain — James I. — Old Descriptions — The Parliamentary Army — Charles I. a Prisoner — His Burial — Examination of his Remains in 1813 — Cromwell at Windsor — The Alterations under Charles II. — The Star Building — Pepys at Windsor — The Pope's Nuncio — The Duke of Gloucester's Death — Improvements under William III. — Queen Anne.

THE first contemporary view of Windsor Castle with any pretensions to exactness was made by Norden for James I. It was among the Harleian Manuscripts, and is preserved in the British Museum, but a very careful copy of it forms the frontispiece to Messrs. Tighe and Davis's volumes on the 'Annals of Windsor,' a work of astonishing accuracy, fulness, and, it must be allowed, dryness, to which I have had constant recourse in the foregoing chapters. Norden's view shows the Castle as it was left by Queen Elizabeth, who had made it a frequent place of residence, sometimes remaining all the autumn, and over Christmas. In 1593 she here translated Boethius's 'De Consolatione Philosophiae,' beginning it on the 10th October and finishing it on the 5th November; or as Bowyer, the Keeper of the Records at the Tower, wrote to her, 'Accompting twoo houres only bestowed every day one with another in the translating, the computation falleth out that in fowre and twenty houres your Majesty began and ended your translation.' There were certain days when she 'rode abroad,' and so 'did forbeare to translate,' for Queen Elizabeth was fond of hunting. In an old view in Braun's 'Civitates' a deer is seen pursued by hounds along the slopes. Although this view is very interesting it is evidently not nearly as correct as Norden's, which I have mentioned above, but it supplies one missing link in the history of the place, for it shows a wooden fence along the summit of the escarpment on the north side, while Norden's view shows the stone wall by which Queen Elizabeth formed the Terrace. The same Queen's new building, which is now the Royal Library, is also seen. The beautiful oriel windows of this addition remind the visitor of the contemporary gallery at Haddon Hall, and show one of the last expiring efforts of the old Gothic school of architects. This range of building is the oldest now visible above ground in the Upper Ward. The dining-room or pavilion which Elizabeth built was at the eastern end of her new terrace, and was an octagon twenty-two feet in diameter. As she did not spend much at any time on building, it is surprising to learn that at least 1000*l.* a-year was laid out in improvements at Windsor between 1569 and 1577.

In Norden's view, and in others down to the Wyatville period, the buildings on the north or Terrace side of the Upper Ward surround several small courts. On the south side of this block, facing the great open space, is the Hall, nearly on the site of the present St. George's Hall. It had probably a fine row of large windows towards the south, but in Norden's view, which is taken from the north, we only see a row of dormers in the roof, and two louvres. The other sides of the Upper Ward are formed of narrow buildings with towers at intervals, and there is no archway as now leading to the Park on the southern side. The centre of the Ward is occupied by an odd-looking fountain, out of which a dragon seems to rise. This 'conduit, as it was called,' was supplied with water from Blackmore, five miles off, and was set up by Queen Mary. The accounts for the work are still extant. The dragon, which was thirteen feet in height, was flanked by five 'Beasts Royal,' namely, the eagle, the 'lyon,' the 'antilop,' the greyhound, and the 'griffith.' Beyond the fountain, on the south side of the Ward, are the 'Lodginges for the Howshold;' and nearly where King George the Fourth's Gateway is now, we see a small arch adjoining a large tower, and labelled 'Sowthe Porte.' The tower of Henry III. in the Lower Ward is described as 'The Lieutenant's Lodging.' Between it and the 'Gate coming out of the Towne,' are the 'Poore Knightes' Lodginges,' the last bay before reaching the archway being marked as the Colehouse, already mentioned as a prison. The Salisbury Tower is named 'The Steward's Lodging.' The Bell Tower has a curious turret, with a cupola rising from the roof. The Horse Shoe Cloisters surround 'The Kewe.' The roof of St. George's Chapel shows four lofty cupolas, one at each side of the west front, and one on each of the transepts. The 'Prebend's Lodgings' overlook 'A Breache in the Wall,' very near where are now the Hundred Steps.

Queen Elizabeth's literary tastes have been mentioned, but it is only tradition which makes her desire to see 'Falstaff in love,' or to command Shakespeare to write the 'Merry Wives.' Still there is nothing improbable or impossible in the story, which I shall have occasion to mention again.

KING JOHN'S TOWER.

Elizabeth's last visit to Windsor was in the autumn of 1602.

One of the first acts of James on his coming into possession of Windsor was to go to law with the

Dean and Chapter. He required them in 1603 to repair the breach in the wall mentioned above. They pleaded that the wall was more ancient than their foundation, that it was part of the outer defences of the whole Castle, and that they were expressly discharged from repairs of the Castle by the charter granted them by Edward III.* The Barons of the Exchequer heard the case in 1606 at Serjeants' Inn, and gave judgment against the King; but he delayed to carry out the work until about ten years later, when, with the help of 10*l.* given as a bribe to a nobleman of the court, a patch, still discernible, was made by the royal orders.

There are several old descriptions extant of the Castle at this period. Among the Harleian Manuscripts is one which Messrs. Tighe and Davis attribute to Stow. It is very much in his style. It contains the story already mentioned as to the building of the Upper Ward by Edward III. out of the ransoms of the French and Scottish kings, and a description of the buildings and surrounding scenery. Having spoken of the buildings of the Upper Ward a making it 'almoste fower sqware,' he goes on to describe the Terrace :—

'Upon the northe syde and uttar parte of whiche

lodgings also, betwene the same and the browe or fall of the hill which is very stepe and pitche, is an excellent walke or baye, rennynge all along the sayd buyldyngs and the syd of the castell borne upp and susteyned with arches and botereres of stone and timber rayled brest highe which is in lengthe 360 paces and in bredthe 7 of suche an excellent grace to the beholders and passers by lyenge open to the syght even afarre of; that the statelynes, pleasure, beautie and use thereof semethe to contend one with another which of them shuld have the superioritie.'

A good deal of fine writing has been spent on the Terrace in the three centuries which have probably elapsed since this was composed, but it has yet to be excelled. It was written in the age of Shakespeare and Spenser.

The interior of the Castle is described by Paul Hentzner, who was in England shortly before Queen Elizabeth's death. He speaks of two bath-rooms ceiled and wainscoted with looking-glass; of seeing the chamber in which Henry VI. was born; of Queen Elizabeth's chamber, in which was a table of red marble with white streaks; of a gallery everywhere ornamented with emblems and figures; of a collection of royal beds, comprising those of Henry VII. and his queen, of Henry VIII. and Anne Bullen, and of Edward VI., all of them eleven feet

FIREPLACE IN THE LIBRARY.

square, and covered with quilts shining with gold and silver. He also saw tapestry, the horn of an unicorn, worth 10,000*l.*, a bird of Paradise, and a cushion most curiously wrought by Queen Elizabeth's own hands.

There is little to connect James I. with Windsor, and though Charles I. projected many improvements, they were never carried out. Among them was a design for making a royal vault under the Tombhouse, a project which probably suggested the chapel as his burial-place. Windsor was occupied by the Parliamentary army as early as 1642, and in the following year fifty-five political prisoners were lodged in the Castle, of which Colonel Venn was the commandant. He it was, who, contrary to the orders of the Parliament, despoiled the chapel, while his soldiers destroyed the deer in the Great Park, and even killed a keeper. We find 'Colonel Cromwell' at Windsor in 1645, and in 1647 Charles is back in the palace of his ancestors, but as a prisoner.

He had still, however, some liberty allowed him, and visited at Latimer's and other places in the neighbourhood before he was removed to Hampton Court. After his escape from Hampton Court and subsequent imprisonment at Carisbrook he was brought back to Windsor in close custody, arriving there on the 21st December, 1648. His arrival led to serious riots in the town of Windsor, where some people were killed. Colonel Whitchcott, then and long afterwards the governor of the Castle, was allowed 20/. a-day for his expenses. On the 19th January Charles was removed to London to return no more alive.

After his execution at Whitehall his body was embalmed and placed in a coffin covered with black velvet, and carried to St. James's Palace, where an outer coffin of lead was provided. Herbert, his attached and faithful servant, applied to the Parliament for leave to bury the corpse in the chapel of Henry VII. at Westminster. This was refused, as it was feared that 'infinite numbers of persons' would be attracted to his grave. Finally, on the 7th February, it was ordained that the body 'should be buried at Windsor in a decent manner, provided that the whole expense should not exceed five hundred pounds.' Four noblemen, Richmond, Hertford, Southampton, and Lindsay, obtained permission to attend the funeral, but were not allowed to do so publicly; and on the evening of the same day a hearse, driven by the King's old coachman, and

attended by four of his servants, conveyed the coffin to Windsor, where it was deposited in what had been his bedchamber. The next day it was removed to the Dean's Hall, which was darkened, and two lighted candles were placed on the coffin. About three in the afternoon the lords mentioned above, accompanied by Bishop Juxon, who had attended the King on the scaffold, applied to the Governor of the Castle, showing him their permit. He would not allow them to use the Service in the Common Prayer-book, and they sadly went to choose the place of entombment. A grave had already been dug on the south side of the Communion-table, but they were anxious that the burial should be in a vault, and, as was mentioned in the last chapter, there are several varying accounts as to how they found the tomb of Henry VIII. When they had ascertained that there was room for another coffin they returned to the Hall, and prepared a piece of lead, on which the Duke of Richmond wrote the words, 'King Charles, 1648.' It will be remembered that the year was then reckoned to end on the 25th of March. The following day the body was brought out and carried round to the western entrance of the chapel. 'It was then observed,' says

Wood, 'that at such time as the King's body was brought out from St. George's Hall (several of the accounts name St. George's Hall instead of the Dean's) the sky was serene and clear, but presently it began to snow, and the snow fell so fast that by the time the corpse came to the west end of the Royal Chapel the black velvet pall was all white, the colour of innocency, being thick covered with snow.' The coffin was placed on two trestles in the vault, 'the head lying opposite the eleventh stall, on the sovereign's side.' The velvet pall was thrown in upon it. 'Thus went the White King to his grave in the 48th year of his age,' without any ceremonial or service, and the Governor, having seen to the closing of the vault, locked up the chapel and took away the keys.

A funeral so private naturally gave rise to the most extraordinary stories, and the burial-place was often asserted to be at Whitehall, and even at Tyburn, but in 1813 the Prince Regent, the Duke of Cumberland, and some other authorities, with Sir Henry Halford, the Court physician, opened the vault of Henry VIII., where four coffins were found. They were those of Henry himself and Jane Seymour, a child of Queen Anne, and Charles I. They

England's mission and India's need."

Speaking of the opportunities for chivalry and self-sacrifice, the Viceroy said :—

"Numerous cases of devotion amounting to the loftiest heroism have been brought under my notice. I have heard of Englishmen dying at their posts without a murmur. I have seen cases where the entire organization of a vast area and the lives of thousands of human beings rested upon the shoulders of a single individual, labouring on in silence and solitude while his bodily strength was fast ebbing away. I have known of natives who, inspired by this example, have thrown themselves with equal ardour into the struggle and unmurmuringly laid down their lives for their countrymen. Particularly must I mention the noble efforts of the missionary agencies of various Christian denominations. If ever there was an occasion in which their local knowledge and influence were likely to be of value, and in which examined the coffins of both the Kings. The body of Henry VIII. was a mere skeleton, a little of the beard only remaining on the chin. Sir Henry Halford's account of the head of Charles I. is well known.

'It was found to be loose, and without any difficulty was taken up and held to view. It was quite wet, and gave a greenish-red tinge to paper and to linen which touched it. . . . The hair was thick at the back part of the head, and in appearance nearly black. A portion of it, which has since been cleaned and dried, is of a beautiful dark brown colour; that of the beard was a redder brown. On the back part of the head it was no more than an inch in length, and had probably been cut so short for the convenience of the executioner, or perhaps by the piety of friends soon after death, in order to furnish memorials of the unhappy King. On holding up the head to examine the place of separation from the body, the muscles of the neck had evidently retracted themselves considerably, and the fourth cervical vertebra was found to be cut through its substance transversely, having the surfaces of the divided portions perfectly smooth and even, an appearance which could have been produced only by a heavy blow inflicted with a very sharp instrument.'

The complexion was found to be dark and discoloured, the cartilage of the nose was gone, the left eye was seen only for a moment, yet the spectators recognised the strong resemblance to coins, busts, and especially the portraits by Vandyck.

Oliver Cromwell seems to have liked Windsor, and in 1654 he caused the Little Park, which had been sold, to be bought back. The Castle was eventually settled by Parliament upon the Protector, and the Poor Knights attended the funeral of Cromwell in the Chapel of Henry VII. During the interregnum before the return of Charles II. the Duke of Buckingham was for some time a prisoner at Windsor. Bulstrode Whitelock was Constable during the rule of the Commonwealth, and on the appointment of Lord Mordaunt, he gave him the particulars I have noticed already, in my first chapter, as to the duties and privileges of the office. Strange to say, Colonel Whitchcott appears to have remained at Windsor after the return of Charles, having probably taken a house in the town. The great event of the reign of Charles II., so far as Windsor is concerned, was the remodelling of the State apartments. This work was carried out by an architect named May, who does not seem to be otherwise known to fame. He only carried out the designs of Sir Christopher Wren, to whom the

Star Building is always attributed. It was so called from a colossal star of the Order of the Garter, worked in gilding and colours, on the centre of the north front. The interior was entirely changed, and the present range of State apartments erected. Wyatville afterwards altered the exterior, and brought it into accordance with the Gothic character of the rest of the Castle. Verrio was employed to paint the walls and ceilings, and Gibbons to carve the fittings. The 70,000*l.* voted for a tomb to Charles I. was probably spent in these new buildings, and in the enlargement of the Terrace, which was continued round the east and south sides. The Long Walk was planted, in part at least, at this time. Another alteration was that the prison tower, sometimes called the Devil Tower, and previously the Rose Tower, at the south-west corner of the Upper Ward, was appropriated to the use of the maids of honour. In this reign, also, the lodge in the Great Park, now known as Cumberland Lodge, was built, and, to judge by an old view which is extant, was probably designed by Wren. It has undergone great alteration since, and shows little trace of his hand.

Samuel Pepys visited Windsor in 1666, when he

was shown 'where the late king is buried, and King Henry VIII. and my Lady Seymour. This being done, to the King's house, and to observe the neatness and contrivance of the house and gates. It is the most romantique castle that is in the world. But Lord! the prospect that is in the balcone that is in the Queen's lodgings, and the terrace and walk, are strange things to consider, being the best in the world, sure; and so, giving a great deal of money to this and that man and woman, we to our tavern, and there dined.'

We may pass over the remaining years of Charles II. at Windsor, merely pausing to note that one of his servants, Toby Rustat, erected in the centre of the Upper Ward a statue of the King in bronze, which is now placed close to the Mound, and which cost him 1300*l*. James II., who was fond of hunting, was very often at Windsor, and the Princess Anna gave birth here to a girl in 1686. The child was baptized by the names of Anne Sophia, but died soon afterwards, and is probably the same princess who was buried in the vault of Henry VIII. It was at Windsor, in July, 1687, that James took the fatal step of receiving the Pope's Nuncio; and in 1688, on the 14th December, the Prince of

Orange arrived at the Castle from the west, and here held the consultation which resulted in the flight of James.

During the reign of William III. we hear more of the town of Windsor than of the Castle; but it was here that the little Duke of Gloucester, the only child of the Princess Anne which lived even a few years, was taken ill shortly after his birthday, in July 1700. 'His distemper proved to be a violent Feaver with a Rash. All proper remedies were applied, but without success;' and about one o'clock in the morning of the 30th of the same month he died, to the great grief of the whole kingdom. His death led to the famous Act of Settlement, by which the Hanoverian succession was established. The little Prince was never actually created Duke of Gloucester, though he was known by that title, and was only eleven years and five days old at the time of his death. His body was embalmed 'and remained in his Highness's Bed-Chamber in the South-East Corner of the Great Square Court of the Castle till Thursday at Nine a Clock in the Night, when 'twas brought down the Little Stairs and put into his own Body-Coach, the Earl of Marlborough with Mr. Sayres, the Deputy Governor, and Gentleman of the Bed-Chamber to His Royal Highness, Riding only in the coach therewith.' He was buried at Westminster, in the Chapel of Henry VII.

William III. made some additions to the Little Park, which brought it to the river's edge, and built a brick wall round it. This wall has not long been removed, and the road to Old Windsor, which formerly went all round outside the wall, passes diagonally across what is now called the Home Park. The ground was laid out as an ornamental garden, and had a fountain in the centre, and in the reign of Queen Anne is said to have been planted with trees which represented from the windows above a plan of the battle of Blenheim. William III. completed the Long Walk, and in his last years employed Wren to make a great design for the south side of the Upper Ward in the 'Italian taste.'

Queen Anne received the King of Spain, Charles III., at Windsor Castle in 1703, when ceremonies seem to have been observed very like those described in a former chapter, when the King of Castille visited Henry VII. The room is still pointed out in which the Queen was sitting with

the Duchess of Marlborough when the news came of the victory of Blenheim. It is a little closet, in the building of Queen Elizabeth, and forms now part of the Royal Library. Queen Anne, in fact, made Windsor her principal residence, but does not seem to have done very much in the way either of improvement or repair; but she appears to have been the first sovereign who withdrew from the state and splendour of the Castle to the comparative retirement of a house in the neighbourhood. To this we owe the 'Queen's House' or 'Lodge,' so often mentioned by Miss Burney, which for a time became really the royal palace rather than the ancient Castle. It was situated on the south side of the ditch, very near the place now occupied by the Royal Stables, and had been Queen Anne's residence before she came to the throne.

V.

George III. at Windsor—Madame d'Arblay's 'Diary'—Her Short Sight—Topography of the Castle—The State Apartments—The Queen's Lodge—Court Life—Herschel—Discomfort of the House—The King's Illness—Queen Charlotte at Frogmore—James Wyatt—Sir Jeffry Wyatville—His Merits and Faults as an Architect—The 'Restoration' of Windsor Castle—Death of George IV.

THE accession of the House of Hanover found Windsor Castle in a fair state of repair; but to the First and Second Georges Hampton Court was a far preferable summer residence. George III. never liked Hampton Court, it is said—I know not with what truth—because his irascible grandfather once struck him in that palace. It is said also that he disliked Kew, which is strange, as he made it so constantly a kind of half-way house on the road to London, and always spent a part of every week there when the Court was at Windsor.

The 'Diary' of Fanny Burney, better known to this generation by her later name of Madame d'Arblay, contains an interesting account of Court life at Windsor and Kew. She was in the service of Queen Charlotte, as joint Keeper of the Ward-

WINDSOR CASTLE IN THE EIGHTEENTH CENTURY.

The funeral of Sir Richard Dickeson, who had been four times mayor of Dover, took place at that town yesterday amid signs of universal mourning. Thousands of the inhabitants paid a last tribute of respect, and all the principal business establishments were closed. The funeral *cortège* was a mile long, the magistrates, corporation, and every public body of the borough being represented. The first part of the service took place at St. Mary's Church, of which Sir R. Dickeson had been a warden for the past ten years.

The funeral of the Hon. Mrs. Eliot, wife of the Dean of Windsor, and formerly Maid of Honour to the Queen, took place yesterday afternoon at Steepleton Church, Dorset, and was attended by the Dean of Windsor, his family, and a large number of relatives. The Queen was represented by Captain Walter Campbell. A memorial service was held at St. George's Chapel, Windsor Castle, while the funeral was taking place at Steepleton. The Queen was represented by the Dowager Lady Southampton, Princess Christian by Miss Emily Loch, and Princess Henry of Battenberg by Miss Minnie Cochrane. There was a large congregation, which included Sir Fleetwood Edwards, Colonel and Mrs. Holmes, Lieutenant Hickey, Mr. Owen Thomas, and other officials of the Royal Household, Mr. Alfred Barber, Mayor of Windsor, the vicars of Windsor and Eton, the Rev. G. D. Nicholas, the Rev. H. L. Warneford, Lady A. Marsham, the Hon. Mrs. Wellesley, and the Hon. Miss Montagu. Bishop Barry, Canons Dalton and Gee, and Minor Canons Tahourdin, Hildyard, and Langdon officiated. The opening sentences (Croft), the deceased lady's favourite hymn, "Thy way, not mine, O Lord" (Dr. Horatius Bonar), and the anthem "Blest are the departed" (Spohr) were sung by the choir under the direction of Sir Walter Parratt.

The marriage arranged between Mr. Sam Mendel and Miss Cecil K. M. Pitt, daughter of Colonel Thos. H. Pitt, of Hayle-place, Maidstone, will take place very quietly in town the first week in December.

THE MEETING OF PARLIAMENT.

The Queen held a Council at Balmoral yesterday for the prorogation of Parliament. The Duke of Fife, the Earl of Kintore, and the Right Hon. A. Akers-Douglas were present. It is understood that Parliament was prorogued for six weeks. The proclamation has not yet been officially published, but when it appears in to-day's *London Gazette* it will probably be found that the date is December 10. Early in December, by which time the Queen will no longer be resident in Scotland, a further Council will be called, and the date of the meeting of the new Parliament will then be definitely fixed.

robe, for five years all but ten days, a period which includes the trying scenes of the King's first illness, her account of which is indeed the most curious part of her memoirs. As she was born in 1752 she was just thirty-six when she first attended at Windsor; and the celebrity she had obtained as the author of 'Evelina,' a novel which is still read and admired, had brought her into contact with the great literary circle of Dr. Johnson. Her father, a musician, was engaged on a history of his own art. Sir Joshua Reynolds was her particular friend, and for a time, when her father had a house in St. Martin's Street, Leicester Square, her near neighbour. Her mind was thus turned and prepared to take an interest in every subject likely to be presented to it—music, art, literature, and even politics. This is the great merit of her 'Diary;' for she was, as a practised writer and observer of character, eminently fitted to describe what she saw, though far 'too good for her place;' and it is with a feeling of something like shame that we read of the insults which her unequal yoke-fellow, Mrs. Schwellenberg, heaped upon her, and find that part of her duty was to mix the Queen's snuff.

But there is one great fault in Madame d'Arblay's

'Diary.' I do not think I have ever seen it mentioned in the numerous criticisms of her work which have been published. There is no background. She, in the first place, assumes that her readers know all about the topography of the places she mentions, and she then shows her own complete ignorance of it. This may be accounted for by her near-sightedness. She mentions it herself in one place, where she says, 'It is almost inconceivable the inconvenience I suffer .... from my inability to confide in my own sight.' She evidently could see nothing that was not close to her eyes. Thus on one memorable occasion in Kew Gardens she nearly ran against the King and his keepers when he was taking exercise. Once only does she tell us anything topographical of Windsor. In October, 1788, she writes of her morning walk that it was in the Little Park—there is not a word as to the view of the Castle from the north—she could not see it—'and to Old Windsor, and round the Park wall, and along the banks of the Thames, and almost to Beaumont Lodge, and in the avenue of the Great Park.' Here, so slight is her geographical faculty, that she goes over the ground in part twice. Evidently she started by descending the Slopes to the

Little Park; she then went out, and skirted the wall of William III., keeping outside, and so to Old Windsor, returning through the Long Walk.

This want of a background makes her 'Diary' very puzzling, if we read it with a view to realising in our own minds what the Georgian Windsor was before the days of Wyatt and Wyatville. As a matter of fact, the whole scenery of Fanny Burney's adventures has disappeared. When George II. died he left the Castle in a very dilapidated state. The Round Tower was falling down, the roof was ruinous, and only the expenditure of the munificent sum of 200*l.* staved off the destruction of the stairs leading to the battlements. There were a few guns, but all the carriages were unserviceable, and most of them were dismounted. The State-rooms seem to have been kept in repair, but in the rare visits of the Court the King must have been most inconveniently lodged. Close under the Castle was Frogmore, the seat of Sir Edward Walpole. The Ranger's Lodge was inhabited by the Duke of Cumberland, who made it a handsome house, and, though it has been much altered, it is still called after him. 'Many gentlemen and families of Estate,' says Pote, writing in 1749, 'constantly reside either in the town, or in lodgings in the Castle, during the absence of the Royal family.' The Upper and Lower Wards presented a very different aspect to that they wear now. Red-brick houses of various dates were in odd corners. The Horse Shoe Cloisters were plastered and whitewashed and otherwise disguised. The 'Standard' public-house stood close to the Deanery. The borough gaol stood close to the Castle-gate. Any official could let his lodgings, and some were absolutely let on lease.

There is a full description of the State Apartments in Pote's book, and especially of the allegorical designs of Verrio, with which walls and ceilings, and even in places the exterior, were painted. The usual entrance from the Upper Ward led through a handsome vestibule in the Ionic style. The great staircase was painted with scenes from Ovid's 'Metamorphoses,' Apollo and Phaeton appearing in the dome. The ball-room was hung with tapestry, which represented the seasons of the year; and on the ceiling Charles II., as Perseus, delivered Europe, as Andromeda, from oppression. In one chamber were the celebrated Windsor beauties, now at Hampton Court, of which Pote observes, 'These ladies are originals, and drawn to great perfection by Sir Peter Lelly.' In the Queen's closet was the banner of France, annually presented by the Duke of Marlborough. In Queen Elizabeth's building was the Picture Gallery, now the Royal Library, and in one of its recesses was Queen Caroline's extensive and curious collection of china. The finest room in this part of the Castle was St. George's Hall. It was ceiled, and the ceiling painted with allegories, among which was to be seen the Cross of the Garter, surrounded by Cupids and the nine Muses. The Hall was 108 feet long by 33 wide, and the whole north side was taken up with a series of wall-paintings representing the triumphs of the Black Prince. The King's private chapel adjoined the Hall, and contained closets hung with crimson velvet; and there was much carved work by Grinling Gibbons, 'representing great variety of palms, doves, pelicans, and other allusions to Scripture history.' The chapel was calculated, we are told, to strike the spectator with veneration and surprise.

There were two or three inner courts in this block of buildings, the largest being the Horn Court, so called from a pair of stag's horns of great size which were hung up in it. The walls were painted in bronze and stone colour, with representations of King David, Jupiter, Neptune, and battles of the Greeks and Romans. The present Waterloo Gallery occupies the site. From the eastern side a flight of steps led up to the King's Guard Chamber, and over them was a dome and lantern, for the painting of which Kent received 200*l*.

Eighteen years after the accession of George III. the Castle was pronounced practically uninhabitable. Various expedients were proposed, and finally it was resolved to keep what remained from actual ruin, but to build, on the site of Queen Anne's Lodge, a suitable palace. The new building faced the South Terrace, and is represented in an engraving by Fittler after Robertson in 1783, a year after its completion as a long, narrow building with battlements, facing north towards the old towers of the Castle, and south towards a walled garden, at the further end of which was the Lower Lodge, a smaller building of similar character, placed on the site of a house in which the Duke of St. Albans had resided in the previous reign, and which George III. bought for the use 'of the younger branches of the royal family.' So much had the Castle been invaded by lodgers and others, that even the slope of the ditch on this side from the entrance to the terrace by a flight of steps and an iron gate, to the gateway of Henry VIII., was let on lease as a market garden. Such was 'Windsor Castle' when Fanny Burney came into the service of Queen Charlotte in July, 1786.

As I have already observed, Madame d'Arblay gives us very little information of a topographical kind, but with the notes here pieced together it is quite possible to supply a background to her figures. From what she tells us of her apartment, it must have been at one of the corners of the Queen's House, probably the eastern. It faced the Castle and the 'venerable Round Tower.' At eight o'clock every morning the King and Queen went across to the private chapel in the Castle to prayers. In the afternoons the younger princesses, with their attendants, went to an apartment of the Castle, where they waited for the King and Queen and their elder sisters, and all went out to walk upon the terrace. To this formality, which is carefully represented in Fittler's engraving above mentioned, the inhabitants of Windsor were freely admitted. Access to the terrace could be had either by the steps and the gate, or through the Castle. 'To avoid the high steps leading to the terrace from the lodge,'

Miss Burney and Mrs. Delany 'went through a part of the Castle.' The wind was high, and they sheltered themselves 'in a sort of alcove.' This was probably at the south-eastern corner, where, in Pote's map, there is a projection in the terrace wall; or else at the north-eastern, where the terrace was extended towards the east over the escarpment, and was furnished with a sun-dial and with a flight of steps which led down into the south garden.

There is an anecdote worth repeating about this sun-dial, which still stands on the Terrace. One day, in the summer of 1787, the King and his favourite son, the Duke of York, had walked for some time up and down the Terrace in conversation, when the King, being tired, stopped and leaned his arms on the dial. A sentry immediately came forward and respectfully, but firmly, told his Majesty that it was part of his duty to prevent any person from touching the sun-dial. The King, instead of showing displeasure, commended the soldier to the favourable notice of his colonel, and he was shortly afterwards promoted.

In the garden behind the Queen's Lodge 'Mr. Herschel, by the King's command, came to exhibit to his Majesty and the Royal Family the new comet lately discovered by his sister.' The discomforts of the house in winter are amusingly described by Colonel Goldsworthy, with whom and also with a Major Price Miss Burney seems to have carried on mild flirtations. 'Let's see, how many blasts must you have every time you go to the Queen? First, one upon your opening your door; then another as you get down the three steps from it, which are exposed to the wind from the garden-door downstairs; then a third as you turn the corner to enter the passage; then you come plump upon another from the hall-door; then comes another, fit to knock you down, as you turn to the upper passage; then just as you turn towards the Queen's room comes another; and, last, a whiff from the King's stairs, enough to blow you half a mile off.'

Every evening the King had music in a concert-room, chiefly Handel; and when Mrs. Delany chanced to be with Miss Burney we hear of the King coming in and taking her away to hear the performance. There is a momentary glimpse of the interior of the room in 1788, where, at the beginning of the King's first attack, the Prince of Wales and his brother, and a number of equerries, doctors, and others, are sitting up in it all night, while the poor

King raves up and down an adjoining chamber, and will not be restrained from making occasional excursions, and addressing wild accusations of neglect to some one of his attendants, to be led off, almost forcibly, at last by the only one of them—a Mr. Fairly—who seems to have showed any tact or strength of mind.

Madame d'Arblay also tells of the visit of the Governor, the Duke of Montagu. He was really Constable, and as such had apartments; but as he was old he did not inhabit them, because it involved more attendance and standing in the royal presence than he could bear. There were special apartments also for the Prince of Wales, and during the King's illness we hear that, not to disturb him, the Prince and his brother, the Duke of York, established a table in their lodgings in the Castle, from which we may infer that previously even the royal kitchen had ceased to be used.

The King's removal to Kew, when the want of privacy at the Queen's Lodge showed that it would be impossible for him to have the requisite amount of open air and exercise, gives Madame d'Arblay occasion for a scrap of local description. It seems that a public road ran between the Lodge and the Castle, and the garden at the back was visible to spectators on the terrace or the tops of the adjacent houses in the town, and crowds assembled to see him depart. 'Almost all Windsor was assembled round the rails.' It was the same when he returned in 1789: 'All Windsor came out to meet the King.'

From this time the Queen's Lodge was the chief royal residence, and the King showed no distinct symptoms of any return of his old malady till after the death of his favourite daughter, the Princess Amelia, in 1810. Meanwhile, however, some attention had been paid to the decaying condition of the ancient Castle, and in 1800 a new staircase, instead of that of Charles II., was constructed by James Wyatt, who had been appointed Surveyor four years before. At the same time some of the old royal apartments on the ground-floor, looking upon the North Terrace, were restored and fitted for the King's occupation. On the final attack of his old malady, he was removed hither, and passed in them the dreary remainder of his life, old, blind, and doting. It is said that he never lost his memory, and on one occasion some attempts were made to interest him in public affairs, but it resulted in increased cerebral irritation. He dressed and undressed himself almost to the last, and spent the weary hours playing Handel on a harpsichord until he became too deaf. Here, in 1820, he died, aged nearly eighty-two, having survived Queen Charlotte a year and a month. A curious print is extant, said to have been engraved from the description of a sentinel who, while on guard on the North Terrace, peeped through the windows and saw the aged King, with his long white beard and his closed and sightless eyes. He was laid to rest under the chapel at the east end of St. George's, where, in 1810, he had caused a vault to be made for the interment of his beloved daughter, Amelia, thus fulfilling a project as old as the time of Charles I., if not of Henry VII.

Good Queen Charlotte, as she was often called, had long deserted the Upper Lodge, and lived at Frogmore, where she had some years before bought the house from Mrs. Egerton,—who had succeeded the Walpoles,—and an adjoining farm. Wyatt was employed to improve the house, and Major Price, mentioned above, laid out the gardens. It was settled on the princesses, her daughters, and after her death was inhabited for many years by Princess Augusta, who survived, unmarried, till 1840. Queen

T. M. — 22 Oct 1900

COLONEL F. C. MAUDE, V.C.

We record with regret the death of Colonel Francis Cornwallis Maude, C.B., V.C., Military Knight, which took place at Windsor Castle late on Friday evening. Colonel Maude was returning about 11 o'clock to his home on the lower ward when he suddenly fell down upon the greensward near the Garter House, the residence of Mr. Collmann, her Majesty's Inspector of the Palace. A couch was at once brought from the Tower and upon this Colonel Maude was laid while Mr. Fairbank, surgeon to the Royal Household, was sent for. Life, however, was found to be extinct, death having ensued from an attack of *angina pectoris*, and the Colonel was accordingly removed to his house a few yards further on. Colonel Maude was the eldest son of Captain the Hon. Francis Maude, R.N. (son of the first Viscount Hawarden), who greatly interested himself in the foundation of the Shipwrecked Mariners' Society. He was born October 28, 1828. Colonel Maude had a brilliant military career. He took a prominent part in the suppression of the Indian Mutiny and commanded the Royal Artillery throughout the operations with General Havelock's column in 1857, including the defeat of the rebels at Futtehpore, the actions of Aoung, Pandoo Nuddee, Cawnpore, Oonao, Busseerutgunge, and Mungarwar, and the relief and defence of the Residency at Lucknow. He was with Outram's force at the Alumbagh from January till March, 1858, and he was also at the siege and capture of Lucknow and was repeatedly mentioned in despatches. He was awarded the brevets of major and lieutenant-colonel and the Victoria Cross; and he was also, in further recognition of his valuable services, made a C.B., and received a medal with clasps and a year's service.

According to the Army List the Victoria Cross was awarded for the following service:—"This officer steadily and cheerily pushed on with his men and bore down the desperate opposition of the enemy, though with the loss of one-third of his artillerymen. Sir James Outram adds that this attack appeared to him to indicate no reckless or foolhardy daring, but the calm heroism of a true soldier who fully appreciates the difficulties and dangers of the task he has undertaken; and that but for Captain Maude's nerve and coolness on this trying occasion the army could not have advanced.—Extract from Field Force Orders of the late Major-General Havelock, dated Oct. 17, 1857."

Colonel Maude was her Majesty's Consul-General at Warsaw from 1876 to 1886, and was subsequently appointed by the Queen a Military Knight of Windsor, first on the lower and next on the upper foundation of that Royal establishment. He leaves a widow and family. His son, Captain F. De M. Maude, is adjutant of the 3rd Battalion Royal Northern Reserve Regiment, stationed at Aldershot.

The funeral will take place with military honours at noon to-morrow in the Windsor Cemetery.

Charlotte died at Kew in 1818, and was buried in the new royal vault. Soon after, in 1823, the old 'Queen's House' was pulled down, and the present royal stables, built in 1839, occupy part of the site. It is, indeed, very difficult to identify any of the landmarks now, everything has been so completely changed. The steps and the iron gate, the railings and the princesses' garden, have all disappeared as completely as the Upper and Lower Lodges. Yet it is impossible, when visiting the place, not to make an attempt to call up the scene of so much that was historically, romantically, nay, tragically, concerned with the lives of monarchs, princes, statesmen, priests, musicians, and novelists, just a hundred short years ago. But, as I had occasion to remark above, the background, or scenery, of Fanny Burney's famous 'Diary' has been shifted, and we can only follow her into what she ignorantly called 'the Cathedral;' and even there, as we shall see presently, almost everything is changed.

Mention has been made of James Wyatt. He commenced the work of 'restoration' carried on, after an interval, by his successor, Jeffry Wyatt, to whom George IV., in August, 1824, gave the name of Wyattville—the accurate Tighe and Davis spell it Wyatville — on the occasion of laying the first stone of a new gateway. In 1828, when the King took possession of the new private apartments, he

NORTH TERRACE AND WINCHESTER TOWER.

was knighted. He continued his work at Windsor through the reigns of George IV. and William IV., living in the Wykeham or Winchester Tower, where he died in 1840.

To Wyatville, as I have already remarked, Windsor Castle owes much. He it was who gave the Round Tower its present height, and improved its outline by the addition of the flag turret. Previously the flag had hung from the summit of the Winchester Tower. The east and south sides of the Upper Ward are entirely his conception. We may quarrel with details, but the effect is unquestionably grand. Wyatville, alone among the early architects of the Gothic revival, shook off the trammels of 'symmetry' which ruined so many fine buildings, and which are but too visible in the design of Barry for the New Houses of Parliament. One of the worst examples of this influence on a Gothic building may be seen in the Waterloo Barrack at the Tower of London. Strange to say, Wyatville escaped this fault, and though his building by no means represents correctly the ideal of a mediaeval castle—which was a fortress first and a residence afterwards—it succeeds in attaining a picturesque dignity unrivalled in England. He built new towers at suitable intervals, he raised the level of all the roofs, he filled up the Brick Court with a grand staircase, and the Horn Court with the fine 'Waterloo Gallery.' The single row of apartments, all 'thoroughfare rooms,' on the east and south, were connected and made habitable by the Long Corridor,—a most happy and successful idea. The brick houses dotted here and there were removed, and the Norman Gate, leading from the Lower to the Upper Ward, had its incongruous additions cleared away. The elder Wyatt had already altered the Italian windows of the building of Charles II., and Wyatville carried out this 'restoration' everywhere except in the Deanery and the Canons' Houses, where we are still able to trace the history of the buildings from the reign of Henry III. He also projected an improvement which it took years to carry out, and advised the removal of the houses in the Castle Ditch. The royal stables were scattered about in different parts of the town. He united them on Castle Hill, and made a commodious and handsome pile in a style to match that of the Castle itself. This was his last work, and he died in 1840 'universally beloved and respected,' as Jesse assures us, adding, 'If Edward III. was fortunate in having William of Wykeham to put his plans into execution, George IV. was not less so in having Sir Jeffry Wyatville to superintend his work of renovation.' This is true enough. Architectural taste at that period was so dead among us that mock Grecian temples, designed with a symmetry which would have astonished and disgusted a Greek architect, were the only buildings in favour. If a design of this kind could be carried out in stucco so much the better, and it is to Wyatville we owe it that Windsor Castle was not rebuilt in the absurd fashion of Regent Street. His details are faulty in many places, but in composition and mass he is unrivalled by any architect of his time and long after. His designs for windows and doors are no worse than those of Salvin, who succeeded him, and who did so much harm by introducing Northumbrian patterns both here and in the Tower of London. In addition to the works already named, Wyatville built the Brunswick Tower at the north-east angle, and the York and Lancaster Tower on the south, flanking the new gateway called after George IV. They give additional dignity to the Upper Ward; but it is impossible not to agree with the oft-repeated criticism that the number and size of the windows destroy the mediaeval effect. Bowles, the Wiltshire poet, complained of the smooth neatness with which the old towers were chiselled and mortared. Had he seen the unfortunate treatment of the Bell Tower by Salvin he would have complained still more bitterly. But, as he justly observes, the distant view is the most imposing.

Another alteration, originally suggested by Mr. Tighe, was the removal of the road to Old Windsor farther from the Castle, and the opening of a new road towards Datchet on the north. Eventually his recommendations were adopted in a modified form, and a new road was made diagonally across the Home Park, the wall erected by William III. being removed; two new bridges connected the opposite sides of the Thames; and new lodges were built. By 1850 Windsor had become in this respect what we now see it; and though some have regretted the old houses in the ditch as adding to the picturesque effect of the old towers above them, few can deny that their removal is a change for the better.

During the progress of the improvements and additions of Wyatville, George IV. lived in a royal lodge near the extremity of the Long Walk. Here he was almost entirely secluded from his subjects. But in 1828, two years before his death, he came to the Castle, and here his long illness detained him till his death, on the 30th of June, 1830. By a curious coincidence, seven years later almost to a day, William IV. died in the same chamber, one enjoying an unusually fine view, even for Windsor; and it is said, I know not on what authority, that in the same room also the Prince Consort breathed his last. It used to be called the Queen's Drawing-room, and is near the north-eastern extremity of the private apartments.

VI.

The Chapel Royal of St. George—The old Chapel of St. Edward—Wolsey's Tomb-house—The Sarcophagus—The Pope's Nuncio at Windsor—The Royal Vault—George the Third's Family—Positions of the Royal Coffins—Some Royal Funerals—The Prince Consort's Family Memorial—The Tomb-house Transformed—The Mausoleum at Frogmore—The First Chapel of St. George.

THE Chapel of St. George has been very frequently mentioned in the foregoing chapters. In its present condition it is pre-eminently regal. No other 'Chapel Royal' can compete with it in this respect. Westminster Abbey, which comes under the same heading, is the nearest to it in honour, as it is the oldest of all; but since our kings have ceased to be buried in the chapels of the Confessor and of Henry VII., it must yield to St. George's. In some respects, too, the chapel at Windsor is older than Westminster; that is to say, while Westminster cannot be looked upon as a 'Chapel Royal' till after the abolition of the Abbey and the practical refounding under Queen Elizabeth in 1560, when it became a collegiate church, the Chapel of St. George was made collegiate by King

ST. GEORGE'S CHAPEL.

ELLISON.—On Christmas Morning, in the Precincts, Canterbury, in his 87th year, HENRY JOHN ELLISON, Honorary Canon of Canterbury Cathedral and Chaplain in Ordinary to the Queen. Funeral at the parish church, Windsor, to-day (Friday), at 1.30. No flowers, by request. T— Fri 29 Dec 99

FENDALL.—On the 22nd inst., at Glenlyon House, Southampton, FRANCES ANNE FENDALL, daughter of the late John Fendall, Member of the Council of the Honourable East India Company, aged 90.

FERRIE.—On the 27th Dec., at The Limes, Upper Norwood, MARGARET FRANCES FERRIE, widow of Alexander Dyce, of Aberdeen and Manila, by her first marriage, and of Peter Ferrie, of Blairtummock, Esquire, by her second marriage, aged 81. Funeral at Outwood.

FIENNES.—On the 22nd Dec., at Malta, CECIL JOHN TWISLETON-WYKEHAM-FIENNES, R.N., Lieut.-Commander of H.M.S. Boxer, second son of the late Honble. and Revd. Cecil Twisleton-Wykeham-Fiennes, aged 32.

FOAKES.—On Christmas Eve, at 76, Cadogan-place, S.W., JANE MARGARET FOAKES, after a very short illness.

FORSYTH.—On the 26th Dec., at 61, Rutland-gate, after 48 hours' illness, WILLIAM FORSYTH, Q.C., aged 87. Funeral Service at All Saints', Ennismore-gardens, 10.30, Saturday, and afterwards at Brookwood. Funeral train leaves Necropolis Station, Westminster-bridge-road, at 11.45 a.m.

FRENCH.—On Christmas Day, ELIZABETH, the dearly-beloved wife of EDWARD HENRY FRENCH, 27, Rockmount-road, Upper Norwood, aged 79.

FROHLICH.—On the 27th inst., at Streatham, WILLIAM FROHLICH, of 10, Sackville-street, London, in his 85th year.

GALBRAITH.—On the 23rd Dec., of hypostatic pneumonia, at 39, Sunton-road, Upper Clapton, FREDERICK WIMBERLEY GALBRAITH, late of the 1st Life Guards, second son of the late Charlotte Britannia and John Murray Galbraith, M.D., M.R.C.S. Foreign and Colonial papers, please copy.

GARFIT.—On Christmas Day, at Bromley, Kent, JOHN HENRY GARFIT, of pneumonia, greatly respected by a large circle of friends.

GEORGE.—On the 26th Dec., at Shortlands, Kent, of acut.

Edward III. in 1348, and the succession of deans and canons has not been interrupted for nearly five centuries and a half. The first Dean, John de la Chaumbre, scarcely survived his appointment six months, but his successor, William Mugge, held the office, which was generally described as that of 'Custos,' for more than thirty years. When John Arundel received the office from Henry IV., he was expressly named 'Dean.'

The foundation was from the first intimately connected with the Order of the Garter, and St. George entirely superseded St. Edward as the patron. It may be said, however, that there are two chapels, and that St. Edward is still commemorated in one of them, for it is quite certain that the eastern building, long known as Wolsey's Tomb-house, and now as the Albert Memorial, is, in reality, except the upper part of the walls and the roof, identical with the chapel dedicated to the Confessor, which was built by Henry III. I have already mentioned that the south wall of the Dean's Cloister is the north wall of the old chapel, and still retains its Early Pointed arcading and vestiges of painting. From the use to which George III. put the chapel when he made it the Mausoleum of his family, it has become one of the most interesting features of the Castle; and when Her Majesty and her children decorated it in honour of the late Prince, they made it one of the most beautiful features as well.

Before King Henry VII. commenced his famous chapel at Westminster, he entertained the idea of restoring the old Chapel of St. Edward, and of making in it his tomb. The work was begun in 1501, but only went on for two years, during which the building of Henry III. was almost entirely removed, and the present 'Tomb-house' erected. The vaulting, however, seems to have been but partially completed, and at a later period we read of a ceiling and of Verrio's painting upon it. It is hardly possible, therefore, to make out with certainty in what state the chapel was when Henry VIII. gave it to Cardinal Wolsey. About 1524 the Cardinal commenced to make for himself a sumptuous tomb in the newly fashionable Italian style. For this purpose he employed a statuary named Benedetto, of Florence, who provided him with a black marble sarcophagus, decorated with figures and statues of copper gilt, among which there appears to have been one of Wolsey himself, because afterwards, when he was in disgrace, he asked Sir Ralph

Sadler to obtain for him his 'image, with such part of the tomb as it shall please the King,' that he might use it for another tomb to be set up in the Minster at York, where he expected to die. His request was not complied with, and the gorgeous metal-work lay neglected in what was then, and long afterwards, called 'Wolsey's Tomb-house.' When Colonel Venn took possession of Windsor Castle for the Parliament in 1642, he very shortly began to cast his eyes upon the magnificent furniture of St. George's Chapel and the plate of the Dean and Chapter; and his successor, Colonel Whichcott, plundered the Wolsey monument, and sold a brazen 'image,' which some have supposed to be a statue of Henry VIII., but which was more probably that of the Cardinal. The splendid character of the ornaments of the tomb may be guessed when we read that even as old brass and gilding they sold for 600*l.*, which translated into modern money represents a very considerable sum. The marble sarcophagus lay neglected in the chapel until 1805, when it was appointed to mark the grave of Lord Nelson in St. Paul's Cathedral. It is sometimes stated that the hero was actually buried in it; but this is a mistake, for the coffin in reality lies within the sub-structure, on which the sarcophagus

AN ANCIENT CORNER OF THE CLOISTERS.

rests. The coffin of Wellington, at his funeral in 1852, was lowered upon it from the church above and there rested until his own granite sarcophagus was ready.

It is impossible not to reflect on the strange fate which has connected the names of two such different men as Wolsey and Nelson. The sailor sleeps beneath the priest's monument, whose own body fills some unknown and unhonoured grave among the ruins of the Abbey of St. Mary at Leicester. His name has lately been placed in the transformed Tomb-house, and his figure, in mosaic, is on the west wall, beside that of the tyrant whom he had served too well. So the world goes round, and Time brings about its revenges!

The Chapel of St. Edward lay desolate for a century and a half. But in 1686 a Romanist was again on the Throne, and the ruin was repaired, fitted, and painted, and some seven hundred pounds were laid out, including the cost of vestments, linen, and candlesticks, so as to be suitable for the restored Mass. The reception of the Pope's Nuncio by James II. at Windsor excited strong feeling at the time, and on the King's abdication the windows of the chapel were broken by the populace, and another long period of decay ensued.

At length, early in the present century, the elder

Wyatt was ordered to inspect the building with a view to its restoration. He took down the ceiling, from which the pictures of Verrio had already almost disappeared. The new roof was not long in its place, for a few years later Sir Jeffry Wyatville took it down in its turn, and revaulted the chapel in accordance with the original design, as indicated by the 'springers' and brackets still remaining. A scheme was formed for making the chapel a Chapter House for the Knights of the Garter, and Wyatt's ceiling was to be decorated with their arms, and even whole-length figures, with heraldic devices. But it was never carried out. When George III. had almost attained the patriarchal threescore years and ten, the death occurred of his youngest daughter, the Princess Amelia—a sad event, which eventually unhinged his mind for the remainder of his life. It was determined to construct underneath the chapel a royal mausoleum. When it was finished at the end of 1811, the coffin of the Princess was privately removed into it.

This Royal Vault, although it is immediately beneath the Tomb-house, is entered from St. George's Chapel by a sloping passage. Through that narrow way his wife, his sister, and six of his children and

THE MEMORIAL CHAPEL FROM THE CLOISTERS.

DOUGLAS.—On the 24th inst., at Kuparra, College-road, Norwood, JOHN MONTEATH DOUGLAS, of Throgmorton-street, London (formerly of Cupar, Fife, N.B.), in his 81st year. Funeral at Norwood Cemetery on Saturday, the 30th inst., at 12 o'clock. No flowers. Friends will please accept this, the only intimation.

DRABBLE.—On the 26th inst., after a short illness, at No. 1, Pembridge-square, Bayswater, ISABEL, widow of the late GEORGE WILKINSON DRABBLE, in her 86th year. Funeral will take place at 2 p.m. on the 30th inst., at Christ's Church, Sandown, Isle of Wight.

ELLISON.—On Christmas Morning, in the Precincts, Canterbury, in his 87th year, HENRY JOHN ELLISON, Honorary Canon of Canterbury Cathedral and Chaplain in Ordinary to the Queen. Funeral in the parish church, Windsor, on Friday, at 1.30. No flowers, by request.

FAIR.—On the 23rd Dec., at Wilderton, Bournemouth, JOHN FAIR, in his 78th year.

FALCON.—On the 22nd inst., at Peshawur, Punjab, India, MINNIE, wife of CAPTAIN ROBERT WORGAN FALCON, 4th Sikh Infantry, and daughter of John Berney, The Close, Croydon, Surrey.

FORSYTH.—On the 29th Dec., at 61, Rutland-gate, S.W., after 43 hours' illness, WM. FORSYTH, Q.C., aged 57.

GILLESPIE.—At Plympton, WILLIAM GILLESPIE, late of Racefield House, Kingstown, Ireland, in the 79th year of his age.

GLOVER.—At 55, Church-road, St. Leonards, CAROLINE EMMA, the beloved wife of REV. GEORGE GLOVER, departed this life on Christmas Day, aged 47.

grandchildren, descended to the grave before the old King himself. At the eastern end, on a low table of stone, lies his coffin, covered with red velvet and surmounted by the crowns of England and of Hanover. His death had taken place but six days after that of his fourth son, the Duke of Kent, whose body was buried in the Royal Vault on Saturday the 12th February, to be followed on the ensuing Wednesday, being Ash Wednesday, by that of his father. A king's funeral was a spectacle unknown to that generation. George III. sat almost sixty years on the throne; and the chronicler of the time calls his funeral 'the most awful and magnificent ceremony which any British subject now living ever witnessed in this country.'

On the right of the coffin of King George is that of Queen Charlotte, and on the left that of his beloved daughter Amelia. Two smaller coffins are at either end. That on the left is occupied by the body of Prince Octavius, who, as his name denotes, was the King's eighth son. He died at Kew in 1783, after having been inoculated with small-pox, at the early age of four. On the right is the coffin of the little Prince Alfred, who died while still an infant in 1782. They were both buried first in the

Royal Vault under the Chapel of Henry VII. at Westminster, and their remains were brought to Windsor at the time of the Duke of Kent's funeral, a few days before that of their venerable father.

The whole vault, the design of which is in the usual Wyatville style of Gothic, consists of a central chamber with arched niches at either side. There is in all space for forty-nine coffins, and the vault already holds twenty. It is twenty feet in length, and twenty-eight in width; and the floor is little more than fifteen feet below the pavement of the chapel above. When the chalk in which it is sunk was being dug out, the bodies of a woman and a child, wrapped in lead, were found, thus showing that the place had before been used for interments. The bodies were evidently those of personages of consideration, but I do not think they have ever been identified. It has sometimes been conjectured that they were the remains of Eleanor of Provence, the widow of Henry III., who died a nun at Amesbury, and of her youngest daughter Katharine, who died a child, and is always said to have been buried in Westminster Abbey, while her mother is stated to have been buried where she died. A little research among the rolls relating to the royal

ONE BAY OF THE MEMORIAL CHAPEL.

expenditure would probably lead to their identification.

On a low slab or table in the centre of the vault lies the coffin of George IV., and near it that of his brother and successor, William, with his Queen beside him. Near George IV., in one of the niches, is the body of his daughter, Princess Charlotte, with her stillborn infant. Probably none of the illustrious dead went to the grave amid more general and sincere lamentations than this first of George the Third's grandchildren. In the niches nearest their father and mother are the infant Princesses Adelaide and Elizabeth, who died before William IV. ascended the throne. The funeral of Queen Adelaide is still remembered by many people now living. It took place on the 13th December, 1849, and the Royal Vault which had been closed since the death of Princess Augusta in 1840, was once more opened. Some of the newspapers of the day published views of the interior, showing the position of the coffins. The Queen's body was borne to the tomb by sailors, but so private were the proceedings that it was remarked that only two persons were in the nave of St. George's during the service, namely, the officers of the naval and military escorts.

From 1849 to 1876 there was no interment in the Royal Vault, for when the lamented Prince Consort died in 1861, his body was only lowered into the passage while the gorgeous Mausoleum at Frogmore was prepared for it. In 1876 a child of the Prince and Princess Christian was buried, and in 1881 a little princess, the daughter of Princess Frederica. Meanwhile, the blind King George V. of Hanover died at Paris in exile, and his body was brought to Windsor to rest 'among his kindred,' as the epitaph on his monument expresses it, on the 24th June, 1878. Last year the vault once more received the body of a descendant of George III., when, amid universal lamentation, the Queen's youngest son, Prince Leopold, Duke of Albany, was laid to rest.

Although the body of the Prince Consort never actually rested under Wolsey's Tomb-house, the old chapel was selected as the site of a magnificent and costly tribute of family affection. The whole interior has been lined with marble and mosaic. The very floor is a work of art. The walls are covered with reliefs representing Christian virtues, and with portraits of the children of the Prince. It would need hours to unravel the full significance of all the

ALBERT MEMORIAL CHAPEL.

1.

QUEEN VICTORIA'S SARCOPHAGUS.

AN UNREPORTED HITCH AT THE FUNERAL.

The sudden intractability of the Artillery horses at Windsor Station was not the only hitch in connection with the funeral of Queen Victoria. There was another and even more awkward one in the mausoleum at Frogmore. The contretemps (writes a correspondent) did not occur under the public eye, and was kept a profound secret by the Court officials and the few workmen who were cognisant of it, but in the neighbourhood of Windsor it has now leaked out that the late Queen's coffin was made too large for the granite sarcophagus in which it was intended to be placed. The mistake was discovered only on the night on which the remains arrived at Windsor Castle. The measurements then taken showed that the coffin was six or eight inches higher than the receptacle in which the Prince Consort's remains rested, and where a space was provided for her late Majesty's body.

The discovery created great consternation among the Court officials and employés at Windsor. Orders were at once given to have an attempt made to deepen the sarcophagus, and stone-hewers were occupied at this work in relays all night. Not being accustomed to work in such a hard substance as granite, and the space being exceedingly circumscribed by the Prince Consort's coffin, little progress was made. There was also the danger of splitting the sides of the sarcophagus. When the granite receptacle had been hollowed out to the utmost extent that was considered safe, it was found that the top of the Queen's coffin would still be six inches above the top, and that consequently it would be impossible to close the sarcophagus.

In this perplexing emergency it was decided, as a temporary expedient, to have slips of wood made, six inches deep, painted to represent granite, and placed on the upper edge of the "walls" of the casquet. On these temporary supports the massive granite lid was laid. The placing of the wooden extensions and the lowering of the lid on them were tried before the coffin reached the mausoleum, and the arrangements were so well made and so carefully carried out that the Royal and other personages who stood round the sarcophagus at what was supposed to be the final scene of the closing of the casquet were not aware of the hitch.

Since then, it is understood, heavy mouldings of granite, from the same quarry in Aberdeenshire from which the stones for the sarcophagus were hewn over thirty years ago, have been ordered by the King. These additions to the sarcophagus have been shaped and polished in Aberdeen, and when completed they will be fixed into the casquet, which will then be permanently sealed. It will consequently stand six inches higher than it did originally.

symbolism. The mosaic which fills the blank western window has been already mentioned. The Prince's ancestors figure in stained glass. The guide-book descriptions of a single feature, the altar, will give an idea of the richness of the decoration:—

'The figures and canopy, surmounted by a cross designed by Sir Gilbert Scott, and executed by Messrs. Poole, are beautifully inlaid with costly marbles — lapis lazuli, porphyry, alabaster, malachite, &c. The bas-reliefs, in panels, are in Sicilian marble, executed by Baron Triqueti. The centre one represents the Resurrection; the one on the right, an Angel embracing the Cross; and on the left hand, Uplifting of the Sacramental Cup. The Altar Table consists of a grand slab of Levanto marble. At the front are three wreaths carved in boxwood; the right hand side is a Phœnix; in the centre a Lamb; and on the left the Pelican feeding its Young with its own Blood.'

The chief and central object is unquestionably the 'cenotaph.' It stands in front of the altar, and supports a beautifully sculptured recumbent statue, a kind of personification of the Christian soldier as described by St. Paul in a well-known passage of the Epistle to the Ephesians. The corners are supported by angels bearing shields of arms, and a figure of the Queen is represented in a panel at the foot. The statue is of white marble, the face being, of course, a portrait of the Prince, whose name with dates and a text is carved round the tomb. A magnificent hound, a portrait of Eos, the Prince's favourite dog, symbolising watchfulness, sits at the feet. The statue and the altar-tomb on which it lies are the most conspicuous objects in the whole chapel, and will probably be more admired in the future than any other part of the new work, which, successful as is the general conception, fails here and there from poverty of design in details. The figure subjects, although the mechanical execution is perfect, are tame in the extreme, with two or three exceptions, which are equally remarkable for extravagance. Nevertheless these are faults which may be mended; the Albert Memorial Chapel remains, as a whole, one of the most splendid monuments of the Victorian age.

It may not be out of place here to insert a brief description of the Mausoleum at Frogmore, where the Prince is interred. It is somewhat of the character of a late Roman tomb at Ravenna, and stands on high brick vaults, to raise it from the damp surrounding soil; for Frogmore, as its name imports, was, at some not very remote period, a

INTERIOR OF THE MEMORIAL CHAPEL.

marsh. There is a central chamber, with four transepts, making the whole monument into a cruciform

ROYAL MAUSOLEUM.

chapel. The exterior, to a height of ten or eleven feet, is faced with Peterhead granite, and polished granite is also largely used in other places. The interior is entirely lined with coloured marbles, frescoes, and reliefs; and in the centre is a large, dark-grey Aberdeen granite sarcophagus, resting on

a base of polished black marble, with kneeling angels of bronze at the corners. These, as well as the figure of the Prince, are by the late Baron Marochetti.

The body is actually within the sarcophagus. The whole chapel is about eighty feet in external height; the central chamber is thirty feet in diameter, and the transepts project about sixteen feet. Altogether this is one of the most sumptuous buildings of its size and kind in Europe. Near it is the smaller mausoleum of the late Duchess of Kent.

Although we know that Edward III. built a great chapel for the religious ceremonies of his newly founded Order, there is not even so much of it left as of the older Chapel of Henry III. The building may have been of a more or less temporary character. The ancient garter-plates on the stalls of the Knights are said to be some of those placed in the first stalls by the founders, but it is far more likely that they belong to the art of the time of Edward IV. The same taste which made the Round Tower such a flimsy construction, and necessitated its being constantly repaired in subsequent reigns, till Wyatville practically rebuilt it, may have influenced St. George's. Certain it is that we know very little about it, except that it was sufficiently large for the 'functions' held in it on St. George's Day. Edward II. had founded a small chapel, with four priests, in the Park; and these, about 1331, were removed and joined with the priests already ministering in the Chapel of St. Edward. Seven years later houses were built for the chaplains on the south side of the chapel. This must have been while the old palace of Henry III. was still in the royal occupation. But some time in 1347 or 1348 the Garter was founded, and in 1353 we have the first mention of a Chapel of St. George. It is evident that no very imposing building can have been erected in the interval; and it was not until the reign of Edward IV. that the glorious structure to which I propose to devote the next chapter was commenced.

VII.

The Chapel of Edward III.—The College—The Knights—
Bishop Beauchamp — The New Chapel of St. George —
Burials — Sir Reginald Bray — Description of the Vaulting
— Some of the Monuments — George III. 'restores' the
Chapel—West's Transparency—Willement's Improvements
— Sir Gilbert Scott's Work — Notice of some remarkable
Deans— Spalato — Matthew Wren.

THE original Chapel of St. George, that in which Edward III. held the first chapters of his newly founded Order, has disappeared more completely than the earlier Chapel of St. Edward. What we see now owes its origin to Edward IV., and it is hardly worth while for us to make any very minute inquiries as to the character of the original building. It was, like the Round Tower, very rapidly and hastily erected. In 1363 the purchase of glass for the King shows that the building approached completion, and in 1365 there are notes of payments for decorations. Thus John, a Canon of St. Katharine's, who is described as 'the King's painter,' receives 13*l.* 6*s.* 8*d.* 'for making a table, whereon images were painted, for the chapel in Windsor Castle.' From John de Lyndesay the King purchased 'a certain table with figures' for the Chapel of St. George. Another man of the same surname was a wood-carver in London, and was largely employed, with others, in making images of saints. The ground occupied was probably the same as that of the choir of the present chapel, but how far it extended westward is doubtful. In addition Edward founded the College, and, as I have mentioned already, appointed John de la Chambre the first custos, whose title was afterwards permanently changed to that of Dean. It appears that the Chaplains or Canons were called the Deans for a time, but in the reign of Henry VI. the present form of Dean and Canons came finally into use; and Edward IV. incorporated them as the 'Dean and Canons of the free Chapel of St. George, within the Castle of Windsor.' There were at first twelve of these Canons. At the present day there are but four, with as many Minor Canons. Besides the Canons the Military Knights were part of the original foundation; but they were afterwards separately incorporated, as disputes arose between them and the Dean and Chapter. They became almost extinct under Henry VIII., owing to want of funds, until Edward VI. granted six hundred a-year for their support. The number was then fixed at thirteen. They were at first known as the 'Poor Knights,' but William IV. changed their designation to 'Military Knights.' Their number was raised in the reign of James I., when Sir Peter La Maire and his executor, Sir Francis Crane, provided money for the addition of five more. The number has since remained at eighteen. The Naval Knights are of private foundation, under the will of Samuel Travers, who was Auditor-General to Frederick, Prince of Wales. He died in 1725, but his bequest did not become available until 1795, when seven lieutenants of the Royal Navy were nominated by George III. Their 'College' is in Datchet Lane, and was completed in 1802. A few years later they received a considerable legacy under the will of Robert Brathwaite, who had himself been in the Navy. The Military Knights wear the uniform of unattached officers in the Army, and the Naval Knights that of their rank. The most curious episode in the history of the Knights of Windsor is, that they attended the pompous funeral of Oliver Cromwell in September, 1658, when we find among their number Colonel Whichcott, whom we have already seen ruling and robbing in the Castle as Governor.

The houses of the Military Knights face the south side of the Chapel, and were originally built for them by Queen Mary, the tower in the centre being the residence of their Governor. The Canons' houses are on the north side, on the site, as I have already said, of the palace of Henry III., and the other officers of the Chapel live in the 'Horseshoe' Cloisters.

The old Chapel, which, besides the installation of the first Knights of the Garter, saw the marriage of Edward the Black Prince to 'the Fair Maid of Kent,' and had the honour of being repaired under the care of Geoffrey Chaucer, was pulled down in 1473, having become greatly dilapidated. Richard Beauchamp, Bishop of Salisbury, was appointed to the office of surveyor. He laboured 'with diligence and sedulity,' we are told; and Edward, considering that, 'out of mere love towards the Order, he had given himself the leisure daily to attend to the advancement and progress of this goodly structure,' made him Chancellor of the Garter, an office to be held by his successors in the See. When Berkshire was severed from Salisbury and made part of the Diocese of Oxford, the Chancellorship went with it, being conferred in 1837 on Bishop Bagot, but on several occasions the succession of Bishops had been

ENTRANCE TO THE HORSESHOE CLOISTER.

interrupted. Sir William Petre was Chancellor in the time of Philip and Mary, and was the first to whom the decoration of a badge was granted. Sir Francis Crane, just mentioned, was Chancellor under James I.; and it was not till the restoration of Charles II. that the office was finally annexed to a bishopric. The duties are not overwhelming, and certainly, since the time of Bishop Beauchamp, no Chancellor has combined with them the work of architect to the King as well.

The design of St. George's Chapel, so far as it was carried by Edward IV., was probably the same as that which Henry VII. completed; that is to say, subject to the changes of fashion, or, as they were thought at the time, the improvements, in Gothic architecture, the credit of the present magnificent and beautiful edifice belongs to Bishop Beauchamp. But at the death of Edward very little had been done, and though the works were continued by Richard III. and Henry VII., it was not until 1517, or 1518, that the Chapel was finished.

Meanwhile its character as a royal sepulchre was established. I have mentioned the graves of Edward IV. and Henry VI.; Pope says of them:—

> 'Whom not the extended Albion could contain
> The grave unites;'

The Garter-plate of cusped form is that of Charles the Bold. In the same stall are the plates of Napoleon III., the late King of Italy, and the present Emperor of Germany.

but they lie respectively on the north and south sides of the high altar. In 1492 Elizabeth (Wydeville), the widow of Edward, was buried beside her husband. The tomb of Henry VI. was esteemed as that of a saint, and there are several notices of offerings at it. Lord Hastings, so barbarously beheaded, without trial or attainder, by Richard III., after a Council meeting in the Tower of London, was brought to Windsor, and buried near his royal master, Edward IV. His widow and son were subsequently permitted to build a chantry to his memory. It was dedicated to St. Stephen, but is still known as the Hastings Chapel, and is situated in the north aisle of the choir. Some mural paintings, illustrating the life of the proto-martyr, are still visible on the walls. Another victim of the short, but sanguinary, reign of Richard lies close by. Sir Thomas St. Leger was beheaded in 1483, and his body was laid here beside that of his wife, the Duchess of Exeter, the King's sister. Their daughter married Sir George Manners, ancestor of the Earls and Dukes of Rutland, whence the name of the Chapel, which, like that which faces it on the south, has the appearance of a transept. Both are in the same style of architecture, and bear the badges and other heraldic devices of Sir Reginald Bray, after whom the southern transept is called.

When, in 1481, Bishop Beauchamp died, and was buried in the north aisle, Sir Reginald Bray, whom we must look upon as his pupil, succeeded him as surveyor of the works; and if the Bishop's devotion to the task of designing and commencing this great edifice deserved the praise of his contemporaries, Sir Reginald is to be accounted still more worthy. Not only did he continue the building for upwards of twenty years, but at his death, in 1502, he bequeathed his lands and money to be spent on the Chapel and on his tomb. The tomb was never made; but the roof of the nave, which must have been nearly finished, is his best monument. The roof of the choir was contracted for by John Hylmer and William Vertue, 'fremasons,' in 1505. We thus obtain the dates for the chief features of the whole Chapel. First, Bishop Beauchamp completed the 'fan-work' vaulting of the side aisles. Next, Sir Reginald Bray and his executors vaulted the nave, the choir being, so far, only roofed with wood. Finally, in the last years of Henry VII., and the early part of the reign of Henry VIII. the choir also received its magnificent

THE HASTINGS CHAPEL.

groining, and the whole of the sacred edifice stood complete.

Of this vaulting a very careful and elaborate study was made by the late Professor Willis, who published the result in a paper, which may be found in the 'Transactions of the Institute of British Architects' so far back as 1842. During the repairs then going on he was enabled to visit the space between the top of the stone vaulting and the outer roof, and made an elaborate drawing of the peculiarities of the construction. According to him, it stands alone among the vaults of the period. I must refer the reader who wishes thoroughly to understand the construction to Willis's paper; but it may be noted here that the masonry is very solid, jointed in large slabs, and so designed as to form a 'wagon vault' of very obtuse angle, so that the central part appears from below perfectly flat. The nave is nearly three times as wide as the side aisles, and the effect was considered by Rickman the richest in England. The choir is rather more elaborately ornamented than the nave, and, as the wording of the contract above mentioned runs, the principal keys are 'more pendant and hollower than the keys of the body of the Chapel.' Some authorities date the fan vaults of the side aisles as late as 1537. The span under the central tower measures thirty-seven feet, while that of the side aisles is but twelve.

Of the monuments a brief survey may not be out of place, but I shall only mention a few of the least known. There are full details in 'Pote' and the local guide-books; and the first thing that strikes the reader is, that so few of the names are those of people of any eminence. It seems that at one time it was quite easy to obtain leave to dig a grave even in the choir. Of course, St. George's did not become the regular burial-place of our kings until a comparatively recent period; but even so, it is strange to find a Mrs. Townley, the wife of a London merchant, buried in 1741, or a Mr. Dent, of Thornbury, in 1634. In the time of the Commonwealth, of course, St. George's was not deemed an exclusive place, and we have such an inscription as this, quoted by Pote:—

'Here lies Charles Cleland.
Triumph with joy. 1657.'

One epitaph is sometimes repeated:—'Dorothy King, lent to her parents John King, Doctor, of Divinitie, Prebendarie of this Chappell, and Marie, his wife, but speedily required again Octob., 1630.' Near it is another on Dorothy's little brother William, who died some three years later, and who, 'being soon

THE BRAY CHAPEL AND OLIVER KING'S CHANTRY.

weary of his abode on earth,' left his parents 'to preserve a memorial of him after ten weeks' pilgrimage.' In another of these miscellaneous epitaphs on obscure people there is a curious example of the old spelling of 'person,' from which one might suppose, at first sight, that George Brooke, 'sometyme Yeoman of the Garde vnto King H. the 8, Ed. the 6, Qveene Mary, and vnto Qveene Elizabeth that now is,' was no good Churchman :—

> 'He lyved content with meane estat,
> And long ago prepared to die;
> The idle parson he did hate;
> Poore people's wants he did svpply.'

In the presence of so many royal and noble tombs it is easy to overlook these humbler memorials, many of which occur also in the cloisters. The whole of the consecrated ground in and about the Chapel seems, in fact, to have been a regular burial-place for people connected, however remotely, with Windsor Castle; and, as we saw in a former chapter, the Castle, until Wyatville's 'restoration,' harboured a very motley crew of sojourners.

George III. made the first attempts to improve the appearance of the Chapel. Unfortunately the royal zeal was not according to knowledge. The 'Gothic revival,' of which we of a later generation have heard and seen so much, had not spread far beyond Strawberry Hill, and the improvements of St. George's cannot be considered a success. Many other churches suffered about the same time, from an idea that stained glass in windows should be of the same character as the transparencies we have recently seen in Gainsborough's 'camera,' at the Grosvenor Gallery. The new decorations were commenced almost a hundred years ago, and continued steadily till 1790, when the chapel was reopened for divine service. The alterations must have been very striking to those who knew the place when it was 'dirty and disregarded to such a degree as to become a nuisance to the eye and a reproach to the sextons,' as one visitor says of it. The stalls and monuments were repaired; a new organ was introduced; the pavement was relaid; but the greatest work of all was the removal of the mullions of the east window and the substitution of a great picture of the *Resurrection* for the old lattice-work. The design was made by Benjamin West, P.R.A., and was carried out by Jervaise, who had done similar work for Sir Joshua Reynolds, at the exhibition of whose pictures last year a portrait of the glass painter was to be seen. But the transparency did not satisfy even its authors. True, Miss Burney goes into raptures about it, but Miss Burney probably never really saw it, for her sight was not equal to the task. In order to try and improve matters, the stonework near the window had to be stained with a dark colour, 'to subdue its bright opposition to the heavy masses of the picture ;' but even this device proved inadequate. Another was tried. The two adjoining windows of the clerestory at each side were built up, and decorated with 'plates of tin, with very indistinct heraldries painted on them.' The same treatment was applied to the panels below the east window, and two additional clerestory windows were filled with the darkest and dingiest coloured glass that could be used. For these Vandalisms West received 1500*l.*, and Jervaise 3400*l.* Willement, to whom a good deal of the present condition of the chapel is due, would have liked very much to remove West's window. The Gothic revival was in full swing in 1844; though, to tell the truth, poor Willement never quite grasped the fact that a window is not a picture. He only, however, obtained leave to reopen the blocked windows, remove the tinfoil, and put up some heraldic designs of his own. He has detailed all his works in the chapel in a well-known volume, and may be said to have first succeeded in

really 'restoring' the original state of things. He repainted and regilt the bosses of the roof, and cleaned the beautiful bay window of the Queen's Closet, at the north side of the altar. It had been painted, probably in the works carried out in the time of George III., to imitate stone.

Meanwhile another serious alteration was made. At the western end of the north aisle was the Urswick Chapel. Christian Urswick was the Dean who rebuilt the Deanery in the reign of Henry VII., and he was presumably buried in his own chantry, which was railed off by a fine stone screen, now removed to the farthest corner of St. George's, near the Lincoln Chantry at the south-east end. The Urswick Chapel was filled with 'the extraordinary monument erected by a very general subscription,' says Willement, 'throughout the kingdom, of unknown amount, to the memory of the lamented Princess Charlotte.' A most extraordinary monument indeed it is. To heighten its theatrical effect the small window adjoining was filled with yellow glass, and the white marble appears to be gilded with perennial sunshine. A statue of the Princess's widower, afterwards Leopold II. of Belgium, has been very appropriately placed close by. It is by

Mr. Boehm, who here comes into competition, by a curious coincidence, with Matthew Wyatt, whose statue at Hyde Park Corner he is about to replace.

The Queen has also erected handsome monuments in the nave and south aisle to the memory of her nearest relations, and to the Prince Imperial, and tablets to the unfortunate young Abyssinian Prince whom our terrible climate killed in 1879, and to King George V. of Hanover. But the greatest work of her Majesty's reign in St. George's Chapel is the removal of West's transparency from the east window and the substitution of stained glass, as we understand the term, with stone mullions, designed, as nearly as possible in accordance with ancient views, by Sir Gilbert Scott. This improvement was effected at the cost of the Dean and Canons, as a memorial of the Prince Consort, and was carried out in 1863. I am not fond of 'restorations,' but even at the risk of falsifying the history of a building I must acknowledge this to be an improvement. The Chapel, and especially the nave, will appear to the visitor too cold and light; but this is a fault which time and stained glass will help each other to remedy. The stonework, which was in a dangerous condition, has been recently renewed

INTERIOR OF ST. GEORGE'S CHAPEL.

where defective, and the construction strengthened, which partly accounts for the look of newness.

This is not the place to enter into details of modern ceremonials, or to describe the gorgeous spectacles which the present generation has witnessed in St. George's. I cannot conclude this chapter, however, without a few words about some of the Deans of Windsor, a complete history of whom would form in itself a curious book. A great many of them have been promoted to the bench of Bishops, and the Deanery of Windsor used to be looked upon as a sure stepping-stone to higher preferment. Oglethorpe, in 1534, was the first Dean who held the office of Registrar of the Garter, an office ever since annexed to the Deanery. Perhaps the most extraordinary of all the list is the name of 'Marcus Antonius de Dominis, formerly Archbishop of Spalato,' who was appointed by James I. in 1618. This strange man was, as we should say, the lion of London society for three or four years, and then disappeared as unexpectedly as he had come. He had been educated as a Jesuit, and while still young had been made a Bishop, and soon after an Archbishop in his native country, Dalmatia. He abandoned the Church of Rome in 1615, and was immediately invited to England, which he reached towards

Gargoyles S¹ George's Chapel

the close of the following year. He was received with the highest respect. Crowds flocked to hear

WINDSOR CASTLE FROM THE BERKSHIRE SHORE.

him preach in Italian. His sermons were translated and published. The English Bishops supplied him with funds until he obtained preferment. This was not long in coming, for he flattered King James, whom he openly compared to Solomon. He was first made Master of the Savoy, and a few months later Dean of Windsor. In March, 1623 (1622 old style), he suddenly made up his mind to recant his recantation. Resigning his English preferments he started for Italy, expecting, at the least, to be made a Cardinal by his old friend and schoolfellow, Gregory XV., who had just been elected Pope. It is asserted by some that he proceeded to Rome 'to confess his faith before the Pope,' and the assertion has at least this element of probability in it, that he may have given it out before he left England. He was arrested and imprisoned immediately on his arrival, and died within a year, whether from disease or ill-treatment is not known.

He was followed at Windsor by Dean Beaumont, who died five years later, and was succeeded by one of the greatest of the whole line, Matthew Wren. When Wren became a Bishop, in 1635, the Deanery was conferred upon his brother, Christopher, the father of the great architect. He fell on evil times, and died during the usurpation. The chief act of his life connects him closely with the history of Windsor Castle. We have already seen how the Parliamentary soldiers treated the Chapel and Wolsey's Tomb-house. One Captain Fogg is described as demanding the key of the Treasury of St. George's from the Dean and Canons, and as threatening to pull the whole place down over their heads. The keys being, nevertheless, refused, Fogg broke open the Treasury and plundered it. Dean Wren had expected some such violence, and had buried certain jewels of the Order of the Garter, but everything else was carried away. A few years later the buried jewels were also stolen, and the Deanery itself ransacked. With great courage and persistence, Wren at last obtained back the books of the Order, containing all its ancient records, and they were thus preserved until the Restoration; but the diamonds and the altar-plate had disappeared for ever.

VIII.

The Town of New Windsor—First Signs of Life—An Unfree Town—Its Troubles—The Charter of Edward I.—The Guild of the Holy Trinity—Windsor in Shakespeare's Time—The Scenery of the 'Merry Wives'—The Town Hall—Sir Christopher Wren, M.P.—St. John's Church.

IN the foregoing chapters there has been frequent occasion to mention the town of Windsor. Apart from the Castle there is more in it than might at first sight be supposed. Historically, the borough, every step in whose municipal progress may be traced, is typical of a large number of English boroughs. From a picturesque point of view it abounds in what artists call 'bits,' though the rough hands of the sanitary reformer diminish their number year by year. And to the student of English literature Windsor stands beside even Stratford-on-Avon in her association with the name of Shakespeare. As to situation, on a promontory round which winds one of the finest bends of old Thames, backed by the lofty Castle Hill, and the wide-spreading park, nothing can be more charming; and now that railways and telegraphs have made such strides towards the 'annihilation of time and space,' people have found out its advantages, and perhaps Windsor may be destined before long to figure as a suburb of London in some future Municipality Bill. In a very few years the area built over has doubled; and all the region round about, Upton, Slough, Staines, Ascot, Egham, Datchet, and many other villages, are growing into populous towns, the paramount attraction being the same to each, namely, the neighbourhood of Windsor.

The Old Windsor of the Confessor dwindled to nothing after the Conquest, and the houses which soon sprang up in that part of Clewer which immediately adjoined the new Norman castle appropriated its very name. As early as the beginning of the disastrous reign of John, there were enough people in New Windsor to go to law with each other. From the names of the pleaders, and the value of the property over which they disputed, we may conclude that they were members of the lower middle class, small tradesmen who lived by the custom which the occasional residence of the Court afforded them. The widow of Simon the saddler sues Hugh the draper for a house worth two shillings a-year; and Robert, 'of the Brick Bridge,' and Alice his wife, become leaseholders of a messuage and its appurtenances. The 'Brick Bridge' was probably that which crossed the Thames on the London road, and connected Windsor in Berkshire with Eton in Buckinghamshire. We have evidence of the importance of the bridge in 1205, when John gave a license to a merchant at Oxford to ply on the river with one boat, and exempted him from toll or 'pontage' at Windsor. The collector was the bailiff. So from this document we gather that the old trade with London by way of the Thames, which had made Oxford prosperous centuries before still went on, that bridges were superseding fords on the King's highways, and, above all, that Windsor had already gone so far towards developing into a corporate town, that she boasted of a bailiff or reeve, who accounted to the King as overlord, or to the Constable of the Castle as his deputy, for the 'ferm' of the town. Among the leases of this period is one of a booth in the Market Place.

Before long Windsor was rapidly rising in importance. A certain amount of protection in troubled times was expected from the vicinity of the Castle. After all, it was better to be plundered by the King alone, than by a lower oppressor and the King himself also, as in other places. Though no fewer than ten horsemen were required of the town during the Barons' War, the great events which preceded

THE CURFEW TOWER.

and followed the meeting at Runnimede benefited Windsor directly or indirectly, as did also the vast building schemes at the Castle of Henry III. In 1242 compensation to the amount of 7*l.* 5*s.* was paid to certain good men of Windsor whose houses had been pulled down to widen the Castle ditch; but in 1256, when perhaps Henry had forgotten the constitutional scruples of his youth, the town had to pay various small sums to an artist who was employed in decorating the new chambers of the palace. This artist, who received two shillings a-day for his pay, out of the neighbouring manor of Cookham, was named William, and was a monk belonging to Westminster. Perhaps we may ascribe the fragments of fresco-work still remaining in the cloisters to William; possibly he was the painter of the beautiful little altar-piece of this period, which now stands near the entrance to the south aisle of the apse at Westminster Abbey.

Although, so far, Windsor could be taxed and oppressed, although it had to contribute men and money for the King's wars, and pay for artists to decorate the King's chambers, it had no corporate existence. Strictly speaking, it was only a hamlet in the parish of Clewer. What this meant in the reign of Henry III., we of the reign of Queen Victoria can hardly understand. Windsor was not a borough 'by prescription.' It had grown up wholly since the Conquest. Other places, that had once been free and were now 'in demesne,' had their traditions at least of folkmote, and had burgesses who fought for their rights, and united in guilds and juries against the common enemy. But Windsor had no organization. The people who dwelt under the Castle were the King's tenants, nothing more, and were governed solely by the bailiff, whom the King set over them. The great ambition of every little town in similar circumstances was to obtain an enfranchising charter. When a charter had been conferred on a borough it became a wholly different kind of place from what it had been before. True, some things were more highly taxed than before, some narrow restrictions were imposed. Still a chartered borough had its liberties. It could elect its own officers; it could assess its own payments; it could impose its own bye-laws; it could regulate its own commercial dealings, in all things saving the peace of the King, and providing duly for the 'ferm,' or rent, which had to be annually paid through the reeve. Nor was this all. The burgesses of a little town which had obtained recognition by means of a charter were free. It required a certain probation, no doubt—a certain apprenticeship, perhaps, before a serf from without the boundaries could become a freeman within; but the man who resided and plied his business in a free borough for a year and a day, and who was still unclaimed at the end of that time by any master or lord, might appeal to the governing body of the town and claim to be admitted a burgess. The admission of such a claim involved payment, and the town was the better. But it may be asked what was the governing body of such a town as Windsor. In the case of some towns it would be very difficult to answer such a question. The governing guilds of London, of Oxford, of Canterbury, of Lincoln, at the period of which we are speaking, were flourishing bodies, no two of them exactly alike, and no two of them with any very distinct point of origin. We do not know how a certain guild in London came to govern the whole city. We do not know when Canterbury received, or assumed, the right to elect her own chief magistrates. But in the case of Windsor there is no ambiguity.

At the beginning of the reign of Edward I. the little town began to be regarded, or at least called, a borough, and its inhabitants burgesses; but they were 'let to farm' by the King, and were held by the Governor of the Castle, who made what he could out of them. Within certain limits, that is, while he paid the King his rent, and while he kept the King's peace undisturbed, he did pretty much as he pleased with the town and the people. Of one constable we read that he purposely left a pasture open, so that the cattle and horses of the people going and returning from their work might trespass on it, and so enable him to impound the beasts and fine their owners. This is only one of several similar complaints against the same oppressor, who paid the King twenty-five pounds a-year for his office, and made it worth thirty. The townsmen were practically at his mercy. It will easily be seen that a charter, which would allow them to elect their own bailiff, which would enable them through him to pay the rent direct, and which would give them the privileges above enumerated as belonging to a corporate town, was the greatest boon they could hope for from any King. They were finally indebted for it to Edward I., who, in 1276, made New Windsor a free borough, the 'good men of the said town' free burgesses, and instituted as a governing body, or, as we should say, a corporation, the Merchant Guild of the Holy Trinity.

Of the subsequent history of the borough there is not much which need be told here. The Guild held its annual 'obit, with mass of requiem,' at the season of Trinity in the parish church; it accumulated a little property, and built itself almshouses; its chief officer was the Mayor, and it returned through him the two unwilling members who were paid forty shillings to represent the borough in Parliament. In all these things there were fluctuations. Sometimes Windsor was under misfortune, as other towns, in spite of the royal favour, and in 1439, indeed, was practically bankrupt. The terrible epidemic visitations of the fifteenth century fell with peculiar heaviness on it. Its houses were unlet, its merchandise went elsewhere, and the various sources of the municipal income, which had formerly been as high as 17$l.$ yearly, were reduced to 6$l.$ 11$s.$ at most. But in a few years things came right, and though the Guild was dissolved at the Reformation, Windsor contrived to lose less than some other places, such, for example, as Birmingham, and in the reign of Elizabeth was in very prosperous circumstances. This is proved by its activity in paving, lighting, and other improvements, and by the building of a new market-house.

To call up a picture of Windsor in the reign of Queen Elizabeth, that is, at the time when Shakespeare wrote of its 'Merry Wives,' is a somewhat difficult task, and has tried several skilful pens. Mr. Jesse, Mr. Charles Knight, Messrs. Tighe and Davis, and others, have left us something more than mere notes on the subject. Yet much remains undetermined; Herne's Oak is as vaguely identified as Datchet Mead, and the Fairy Pit as Page's House. Of the general aspect of the place, nevertheless, we may, perhaps, call up a very correct presentment. The narrow, straggling street of picturesquely gabled houses led up the hill from the steep arch of the bridge; the blue roofs and grey walls of the Castle towering over the red tiles and half-timbers of the town. A cross stands at the top of the hill where Peascod Street leads down on the right and the Castle Hill leads up on the left. Where there is little or none of the vehicular traffic of the present day, the street seems very wide, and for the convenience of the weekly cattle market a stout barrier of timber runs down the middle. Two inns hang out their signs, gaudily painted, near the cross, the 'Garter,' sometimes no doubt called the 'George,' and the 'White Hart.' Opposite, under the Castle wall, is the house of the Fords. A little farther on is the Market House, then recently built, and standing on high arches

WINDSOR CASTLE FROM THAMES STREET.

over the centre of the market-place at the cross. The upper storey forms a source of revenue to the Corporation, as it is let to an inn-keeper for five or six pounds a-year. A little to the left, nearly facing the new gate which Queen Elizabeth has built to the Castle, at the corner of Church Street, is the Town Hall, the seat, before the suppression of chantries, of the governing Merchant Guild of the town or fraternity of the Holy Trinity, and afterwards of the Mayor and Corporation. Still going south, over the shoulder of the hill, we come, beyond the market-house, to the pillory standing ready for offenders, and a little to the left, with green fields about it, the church, its spire rising from a square tower. A hundred yards farther on the houses cease, and we are in the open country, the Park, with its dense foliage, closing in the view on the eastern side, and the river winding away into the distance westward toward Bray.

Such is the background, the scenery, for those passages of the 'Merry Wives' which relate to the town of Windsor. Of those which relate to the Park we may have occasion by-and-by to speak. Not only has everything changed, as in the town, but controversy has raged as to the identity of each spot. To people who are not specially Shakespearian scholars there is something very deterrent both in the futile guesses and the divergent views of students, and also in their absorption in a pursuit which, notwithstanding the number of minds exclusively devoted to it for the hundred years last past, has added hardly anything to our knowledge of the personal history, appearance, or disposition of the poet. That he was thoroughly acquainted with Windsor is beyond dispute. He even knew the names of some of the leading townspeople. Ford and Page are not accidents; both occur in the registers of the time. That he should have used the names of local families for his characters, and should have purposely distorted the local topography, is incredible. We cannot doubt that in his mind's eye he had before him the places he describes: to identify them now would, perhaps, be easier if Shakespearian commentators had not been so busy with their wild guesses for a century at least. The action of Malone, who painted Shakespeare's bust a dirty white, is typical of a majority of the tribe; and each wiseacre, as he has gone over the ground, has so carefully erased the footsteps of his predecessor that the footsteps of the great poet himself

BITS OF OLD MARKET STREET, WINDSOR.

which underlay them all have long ago been obliterated. Charles Knight, perhaps, did less harm in this respect than any other critic, and, moreover, knew and loved Windsor. In his *Studies of Shakespere* (1851) he makes a vehement, if ineffectual, attempt to date the 'Merry Wives;' but he goes on, in a passage of considerable beauty, to sketch Elizabethan Windsor, a quiet, country town, sleeping under the shadow of its neighbour the Castle. He speaks of its gabled houses, separated by pretty gardens, 'from which the elm, and the chestnut, and the lime, throw their branches across the unpaved road,' and he introduces us, one by one, to the 'goodly company' assembled under their shade. But in Mr. Knight's local illustrations of the play in his 'Pictorial Shakespere,' he observes that the period of its action is 'about two centuries before Shakespere's own age,' an assumption in which it is not easy to follow him. Still it leads to a vivid little picture of the appearance of Windsor in the time of Henry IV., from which we gather that the Castle must have still presented the aspect, not of a palace, but of a very strong fortress, for the terraces did not then conceal 'the stern grandeur of the walls standing boldly upon the rock of chalk.' He places Page's house in the High Street, a little to the north of the present Town Hall, and is probably right in believing that there were no houses along the edge of the Castle ditch. But though the Fords may not

WINDSOR TOWN HALL, FROM THE HIGH STREET.

have lived on that side, or in Windsor at all, in the time of Henry IV., this is no reason for supposing they did not in the reign of Elizabeth: and altogether, what with local allusions, what with historical allusions, what with manners and customs, the play of the ‘Merry Wives’ is thoroughly and wholly Elizabethan, and the Elizabethan scenery of Windsor, as it is preserved to us by Norden's drawings, now in the British Museum, suits it best.

Of the late history of the royal borough there is not very much to be said. With a single exception it is devoid of interesting buildings. The Market House has been mentioned above more than once. The old building must have resembled the market houses now or lately standing at Warwick, Leominster, and other places; a wide open space below, supporting on stout oak pillars a chamber above. In 1687 it became ruinous, and about the same time it was decided to unite the Town Hall with it; and a certain Sir Thomas Fitz, the Surveyor of the Cinque Ports, was employed to make the proper design and carry out the building. On the 5th of September the first stone was laid, but Sir Thomas died early in the following year, and Sir Christopher Wren was directed to finish the work. Wren's connexion with Windsor was long and intimate. His father had been Dean, and was gratefully remembered for having saved the records of the Garter during the Great Rebellion. Sir Christopher himself, besides being Surveyor of Works at the Castle, sat for the borough in the famous Convention Parliament which acknowledged William and Mary, the very year he began to work at the new Town Hall. He had trouble about his election, which was annulled by the House, and he was eventually unseated; but his building remains much as he left it, and, we may hope, will remain for a little longer; for as Thorne, who did not admire it, observes, it is the oldest building now in the town, though a private house is sometimes doubtfully attributed to Inigo Jones. The Town Hall was a good deal pulled about and altered, not for the better, a few years ago; but is in some respects a characteristic example of the plain, solid, yet delicately proportioned style of the great architect—a style which, for a few years during the present century, was as little understood by the ordinary architect as Gothic in the reign of George II. The building cost the modest sum of 2000*l.* 14*s.* 4*d.*, another example, like a majority of his City churches, of the small sum a real artist requires to produce a good effect. Wren did not employ excessive ornament to conceal faults of construction and proportion, but by spending a little thought he saved a great deal of money. The day is coming when his unerring canon of proportion, forgotten awhile, will be recognised again; and architects will have to find out, by his example, why it is that granite columns, carved capitals, marble inlay, and the expenditure of vast sums on stucco, fail to make a mean design look handsome. I do not want to over-praise the Town Hall of Windsor; but given a similar sum, in the proportion of the present day, given the same site and the same requirements, and let us ask, is there an architect in England who can produce anything so suitable, so solid, and, on the whole, so picturesque?

An anecdote is sometimes told about the Hall which well illustrates both Wren's character and his method of going to work. It is told by one of his latest biographers, and rests probably on tradition, yet there is nothing in it absolutely improbable. When the Town Hall was finished the Corporation attended to inspect and approve. It was, and is, like the Market House it superseded, built upon tall pillars, which, supporting the council chamber and offices of the municipality above, leave space for the ancient Corn Exchange below. One of the burgesses objected that the upper room was not adequately supported, and Wren undertook to strengthen the lower storey by putting in two additional columns. The objector was satisfied, little guessing that the architect, when the new pillars were erected, left half-an-inch between them and the floor they were supposed to sustain. 'Wren must many a time have laughed to himself when he passed that way.' Miss Phillimore attributes to him three other houses in Windsor.

When the new Hall was finished the inhabitants set up at one end of it 'the Queen's effigies.' For this statue, which stands in a niche nearly facing the gateway of Henry the Eighth, and represents Queen Anne, with all the ensigns of royalty, the town paid 40*l.* in 1706, and a few years later Sir Christopher gave them a similar statue of Prince George of Denmark 'in a Roman military habit,' to set up at the opposite, or southern end of the building. The Corporation accounts contain various small charges for gilding these statues, and for writing bombastic inscriptions beneath them.

In 1835 the old Corporation was reformed, with so many others, under the Act of that year, and since then the corporate body consists of the Mayor, six aldermen, and eighteen councillors, and the old restricted qualifications of burgesses are enlarged to admit all men who occupy houses or shops, and have paid their poor-rate. While they are enlarged in one direction they are narrowed in another, as women are no longer allowed to become free of the borough, as they were previously. Windsor continued to send its two representatives to Parliament until 1867, when a member was taken away.

One other public building must be noticed. The Church of St. John the Baptist used to stand, as we saw above, well clear of the town, and, in the time of Shakespeare, was probably quite as large as the parish required. At the suppression of chantries the Corporation accounts contain an item from which it seems that 'Mr. Mayor' paid for the 'brasen deske in the parishe church to the use of the halle,' ten shillings. This was only part of a large amount of church furniture and ornaments which was disposed of in a similar manner at that time. In 1822 the church had become so dilapidated that a new one was considered necessary. The design was made by a Mr. Holles in what was considered to be fifty years ago the Gothic style. Notwithstanding the thorough remodelling which was given to it by Mr. Teulon in 1869, it remains 'large, light, and commodious,' but essentially and irremediably ugly and common-place. There are several other churches in the Windsor of to-day, but neither they, nor the schools, nor other public institutions, add much, or anything, to the picturesqueness of the royal borough.

IX.

The Home Park—Herne's Oak—Datchet Mead—Datchet—Iver Church—Langley Church, Almshouses, and Library—Upton Church—Salt Hill—Eton College—Gray and Stoke Poges—Burnham Beeches—The Northern and the Southern Environs of Windsor contrasted.

IT seems to be now a settled matter, even in the minds of the Shakespearian controversialists, that Herne's Oak has not been seen above ground during the present century. Nevertheless, a tree, which fell in August, 1863, and which had stood on the eastern side of the Broad Walk, not far from the footpath to Frogmore, was long known locally by the name. In any question which relates both to Shakespeare and to Windsor, the authority of the late Charles Knight stands very high, and he speaks with little hesitation in his comment on the 'Merry Wives.' He was satisfied, both by the testimony of some old inhabitants and his own recollections, that Herne's Oak stood in what is now the Home Park at a spot which he describes as 'a little dell,' now filled up. The oak itself was probably cut down at the end of the last century with several other decayed trees, which were removed by direction of George the Third under some misapprehension. The 'little dell' and the old tree or trees which Knight recollected have alike disappeared. During the alterations which resulted in the diver-

DATCHET.

sion of the footpath to Datchet the dell was made level, the thorns which filled it were buried, and the ancient roots of the old trees which stood in and about it were covered up. 'Surely,' he exclaims, 'the rubbish of the Castle might have been conveyed to a less interesting place of deposit.'

With regard to Datchet Mead Knight was

equally clear. The road from Windsor to the bridge connecting the two sides of the river at Datchet—a bridge which, after existing for some years in the reign of Queen Anne, was succeeded by a ferry, passed across some flat ground below the North Terrace. In the time of William the Third this field was taken into the Home Park and a wall built round it. It thus lost its Shakespearian name, and the avenues of elms planted on it were said to have been intended by Queen Anne to represent the disposition of the allied forces at the battle of Blenheim. Certainly when you look down upon what remains of them from the windows of the Castle above, they do present signs of a somewhat whimsical arrangement. Knight had no doubt that it was in this field, then unenclosed, that Falstaff, according to Shakespeare, was emptied into a muddy ditch beside the river's bank. In the year 1845 Mr. Tighe, well known as one of the authors of the 'Annals of Windsor,'—a book from which I have constantly quoted in the foregoing chapters—made a suggestion that the road between New and Old Windsor should be removed much farther to the south, and the footpath to Datchet, which ran very close under the Castle walls, should be shut up, a new carriage-road nearer to the Thames being substituted. He also suggested the building of the two bridges, and several other improvements, most of which were carried out to the great convenience of the public and the great improvement of the Home Park. But we can scarcely now realise how entirely different was the condition of the Park adjoining the Broad Walk, even at the end of the last reign. At present we can hardly perceive that there is any point of separation between the Park immediately adjoining the Castle and that part of the Great Park into which the Broad Walk leads us. Then, and later, there were long gaps even in the Crown estate, and places had been let off as farms, and even sold as villas. There is a receipt extant in a private collection of historical documents, dated as far back as July 3, 1683, which shows that the project for uniting the two parks by an avenue was already entertained in the reign of Charles the Second; but I must refer any reader who wishes to trace the gradual steps by which order was brought out of confusion and the present admirable example of landscape-gardening on the largest scale was completed, to the work of Messrs. Tighe and Davis just mentioned, and to that of Mr. Menzies on 'Windsor Great Park.'

Queen Anne's bridge to Datchet, after having been rebuilt and frequently repaired, was so decayed in 1795 that it became useless. Various attempts were made in vain to compel the counties of Berks and Bucks to rebuild the bridge, but it was not until 1812 that these efforts were successful. Even then the two counties could not agree as to the design, and each built according to its own pleasure half across the river, the junction being but clumsily effected. The very handsome Victoria and Albert Bridges which now join Datchet to New and Old Windsor respectively, were built in 1851. The views from them are exceedingly fine. Of Datchet itself there is not much to be said except that it contains a fine half-timbered house of five gables. The church is not thirty years old, but is a favourable example of modern Gothic. The ecclesiologist must go a little farther inland for anything of interest, but he will be abundantly satisfied within a few miles by an inspection of Iver or Langley, of Upton or Stoke Poges. There are full accounts of Iver in all the local and other guides, and it is certainly a very handsome old church, and well worthy of a visit for its fine long nave and chancel, its Norman arcades and its very curious monuments.

Among these last there is one which I have not seen noticed. Perhaps it is considered too modern since it only dates from 1813, yet this was the age of 'Marmion,' first published in 1808; and it would be hard to believe that the author of a rhyming epitaph on the young lieutenant Hawkins Whitshed, killed in a naval action, had not the worst but most celebrated of Scott's couplets in his mind. After describing how gallantly Whitshed led his men to the capture of one French ship, it ends by asserting that he,

'Dying, exclaimed amid the battle's roar,
"Carry her if you can, my lads, I am no more."'

We have heard so much of the picturesque aspect of Gray's Stoke, and some people have in the same connexion taken occasion to press the claims of Upton with its 'ivy-mantled tower' to be the true scene of the Elegy, that I am surprised so little notice has been taken of a church and churchyard in the same neighbourhood which most people would be inclined to consider more interesting and more beautiful than either, although no poet has sung of its 'rugged elms,' its uncouth epitaphs, or its 'shapeless sculpture.' Some authorities seem to

ALMSHOUSES AT LANGLEY.

think that the name of Langley Marish contains a reference to the dedication of the church to St. Mary, but to my mind such a derivation is inadmissible. 'Marish' is marsh 'writ long,' and serves to distinguish this one from innumerable other Langleys. The flat, low-lying land, of which a great part of the parish consists, is quite enough to account for it. Within the compass of a very few square yards we have here an unusual number of features of picturesque and historical interest. The churchyard, which in summer is a blaze of flowers, is flanked north and south by rows of red brick almshouses. Those on the south are dated on a stone over the porch, 1617, and were built by Sir John Kederminster. His father, Edmond, was keeper of the royal park of Langley, a part of the honour of Windsor; and in 1626 Charles I. granted the estate to the family. Sir John in 1630 made extensive alterations in the interior of the church, when he removed the pillars and arches between the north and south aisles and supplied their place with a Doric screen so well proportioned that had he not put the date upon it the design might have been attributed to a much later period. His almshouses were imitated on the north side by Sir

Henry Seymour, who was created a baronet at the Restoration, and came to live at Langley in 1666, when he rented the house and park from the heirs of the Kederminsters. He eventually bought the estate, but the date of his coming here is worth noting, as otherwise his almshouses might be supposed much older than they are, and certainly at least a century older than the screen in the church. It is evident that an attempt was made—and a successful attempt—to imitate the style of the Kederminster building opposite. The two contrast unfortunately with a modern schoolhouse, which forms a third side to the little square. The visitor finds it difficult to understand the mental and aesthetical condition of the architect who with two such models before him could have designed this deplorable building.

But Kederminster deserves to be remembered at Langley for a building which is more interesting in itself by far than even his almshouses or his alterations in the church. Adjoining a kind of south transept, fitted up in 1792 for the private pew of the lord of the manor, there stands on the west side a small chamber filled with books. The fittings are carved and painted in a style so singular, yet

VIEW FROM THE TERRACE OF THE CASTLE.

so effective, that at the present day, when architects study so carefully the remains of Jacobean and later Stuart work, it is surprising that Langley is not constantly occupied by students. The carved and painted woodwork is in excellent taste, and almost as fresh as if only executed yesterday. On the inner sides of two cupboard-doors were the portraits of Sir John Kederminster and Mary Gerrard, of Dorney, his wife. Unfortunately, through an injudicious attempt at restoration, the figure of the lady has utterly perished. Both portraits appear to have been painted over, perhaps during the Civil War, but by the loving care of a local artist the features and the heraldic badges of one—that representing Sir John—were revealed once more. Strange to say, the story goes—an excellent example of the difficulty of ascertaining historical truth—that after Kederminster's death, which occurred in 1631, the doorway of the library was built up and its existence forgotten, until so recent a period as 1830. This assertion is made in nearly all the modern books in which Langley is mentioned. Thorne avoids falling into the error, and as the library is mentioned by Hakewill, who wrote in 1813, it was evidently open then, while Charles Knight makes the pleasant suggestion that John Milton may have used the books during the seven long years that he lived at Horton, two miles across the fields from Langley.

The books are for the most part great folios

LIBRARY AT LANGLEY.

of ancient divinity, some three hundred in number. They are contained in five panelled cupboards, decorated with coats-of-arms, the Kederminster badge, an eye and the words '*Deus vidit,*' figures of saints, angels, and prophets, together with a long series of curious little landscapes, representing, among other places, Windsor Castle as it appeared in the reign of James I. The whole chamber is so small that it may be thought that I am dwelling too long upon it, but parochial libraries are very rare in England, and probably no other is of such interest to the artist or the antiquary as this, and, considering its nearness to London, so little known.

A very short way westward from Langley is Upton Church, whose ivy-clad Norman tower has of course given rise to a local idea that it is the scene of Gray's Elegy. It stands in a beautiful churchyard, with all the proper accompaniments of rugged elms and yew-tree's shade. No doubt Gray did not confine his mind to the contemplation of any one church in particular; and it is a curious coincidence that so many churches of the character of that alluded to in the Elegy should be in the immediate neighbourhood. But Upton has suffered from most sweeping alterations and restorations. Its tower has been lowered, but is still ivy-clad. The Norman north aisle, with its rare groined chancel, has been supplemented by a south aisle so closely imitating ancient work that even a fair judge may be forgiven if he finds himself constantly deceived as to what is old and what is new. The visitor will observe with interest the Herschel monument against one of the tower piers. There is a long inscription in Latin in honour of the great astronomer; but it is remarkable in these days when we hear so much about woman's genius and woman's work, that the ladies of England have set up here no memorial of the marvellous powers of calculation and the devoted assiduity of Sir William's sister Caroline, who is also buried in the same tomb. A broken stone in the churchyard on the north side bears an inscription which may be worth noting as suggesting possibly a soluble, if difficult, historical question :—

> ' Here lies the body of
> Sarah Bramstone,
> Of Eton, Spinster, a person who
> Dared to be just in the reign
> Of George the Second.
> Obyt Jany ye 30th, 1765,
> Ætat 77.'

From Upton Church to Slough is but a step, and there, in the grounds of a private house, may still be seen some relics of the famous telescope which was described heraldically in the grant of arms to the Herschel family, thus : ' Argent, on a mount, vert, a representation of the forty feet reflecting telescope, with its apparatus proper.'

A little beyond Slough is Salt Hill, the celebrated Eton Montem. It stands in a field on the south side of the road, close to a clump of very fine elms. Strange to say, the whole ground is advertised for sale for building purposes. The Montem itself seems to be a barrow of the same kind as that which was opened not long since at Taplow. If it is to be rased in favour of a villa or a row of houses we must hope some competent antiquaries will be present, as it is not very creditable to the present state of historical knowledge that the Eton Montem is so constantly referred to as Druidical, and the Taplow mound was so often called the grave of a Viking. The school celebrations, at first triennial, were attended by large crowds of spectators, although, except when the festival was honoured by the presence of royalty, there cannot have been much to see. The collection made for the captain of the school was, no doubt, a serious consideration, but when the railway came to Slough the crowds were greatly augmented, and the whole thing became objectionable. It is now almost forty years since it was abolished.

From Eton Montem to Eton College Windsor Castle is in sight all along the pathway. When the bridge is reached close by the Playing Fields a back view of the old school buildings, although all the grander features of the place are invisible, should certainly not be missed by any traveller who admires harmonious colour—old red bricks contrasting with fresh green vegetation—and the charm of ancient irregularity. Although this is the back way to enter Eton it is in many respects superior to the approach from the Windsor end. The best buildings of the school are seen at once and appear to form a little town in themselves. The first quadrangle has but a mean entrance, although it was designed by Sir Christopher Wren, but as he was only allowed by Dr. Allistree, the head master, to spend 1500*l.* he could not have been expected to do much better. The arcade viewed from the interior of the quadrangle is in excellent proportion. On the right or south side is the chapel, a very fine and interesting building, but incomplete. In general appearance it comes halfway between St. George's Chapel on the hill above and the chapel of King's College, Cambridge. It is possible in a view from Snow Hill at the southern end of the Long Walk to get St.

ETON COLLEGE.

George's and the Eton Chapel into a single line, when the general resemblance, details being hidden by distance, is very plain. The chapel stands on the site of the ancient parish church which was wholly done away with; but the situation was badly chosen, because if the nave, as originally intended, had been built it would have stretched right across the roadway. The troubled times of 'Holy Henry' both prevented the building of anything but the choir and left that unfinished. After just four centuries had elapsed what was called a 'restoration' was commenced, in the course of which some improvements and some terrible destructions were wrought. The roof, which had been covered by a plaster ceiling, was opened with handsome beams. All traces of classical work were swept away; and when the oak panelling was removed a double row of very curious paintings was revealed. They represented the miracles of the Virgin; and, incredible as it may seem, half of them were erased and the lower row was covered by the new panelling on the grounds that they did not suit Protestant worship.

The gateway under the clock which leads to the Green Yard, as the inner quadrangle is called, reminds us of Hampton Court and of St. James's Palace. It is curious that no example of this kind of architecture should remain in Windsor Castle, nor does it seem likely that any of the buildings of Henry VIII. and Queen Elizabeth resembled it. The variety of red brick chimneys is famous, but most of them, I fear, have been removed of late years. Modern innovation has also been very busy among the master's houses, but it is satisfactory to observe that the latest buildings are less incongruous and more picturesque than those of a few years ago. It would be but too easy to linger in Eton College, and few visitors can tear themselves away before they have seen the hall and the library, and perhaps also the pictures in the Provost's lodgings; but when we reach, through a little ivy-mantled postern, from the cloisters, the wide expanse of the Playing Fields—the boys call them the Shooting Fields, which gives more point to the Duke of Wellington's assertion that Waterloo was won in them—we involuntarily think of Gray. The grove, the lawn, the mead,—

> 'Whose turf, whose shades, whose flowers among
> Wanders the hoary Thames along
> His silver winding way,'—

STOKE POGES CHURCH.

are calculated to direct our thoughts to Stoke, of which he also sang, and where he lies buried. Stoke is a very short way off, and may easily be

visited in the course of the same excursion. As Mr. Gosse has well observed, the Eton Ode is redolent of Stoke Poges, and merely to have walked in fields where Gray 'must have muttered his verses as they took shape gives the reader a certain sense of confidence in the poet's sincerity.' From Stoke Gray could see 'the distant spires and antique towers' of which he sang. 'The woodland parish' is full of little rights of way, meadow paths without hedges, skirting the breast of a gentle acclivity, and revealing 'against the southern sky the embattled outline of Windsor.' When he wrote this little poem he entitled it in his first manuscript, 'Ode on a Distant Prospect of Eton College, Windsor, and the adjacent country.'

The church of Stoke would be thought pretty anywhere. No vestige of hamlet or village is to be seen, 'and the aspect of the place is slightly artificial, like a rustic church in a park on the stage.' Mr. Gosse continues in language that seems almost profane in this connexion, yet which is so exactly appropriate that I cannot refrain from quoting it: 'The traveller almost expects to see the grateful peasantry of an opera, cheerfully habited, make their appearance, dancing on the green sward.'

The next parish beyond Stoke to the westward also contains vivid associations with the name of Gray. He it was who discovered Burnham Beeches. Writing to Horace Walpole in 1737, he says that half a mile from his uncle's house at Stoke he has

BURNHAM BEECHES.

a forest all his own, 'for I spy no human thing in it but myself.' This was Burnham Beeches, which must be reckoned as the north-western corner of that part of the great woodland district which rendered Windsor so attractive to our early kings. Although finer single trees may be seen in Windsor Great Park—as we shall have occasion to notice in our next chapter—there is nowhere, as Mr. Thorne well observes, so wildly picturesque an assemblage of ever-varying giant trunks, or such striking combinations of sylvan forms and colours, and endless contrasts of lights and shadows. Jesse, too, was warmed into enthusiasm by 'glens and valleys interspersed with little rushy pools, the winter haunt of the snipe and the woodcock, and overhung with the rich foliage of the holly, birch, juniper, and other trees, under whose shade the purple heaths flourish and the fern and foxgloves add a charm and variety to the scene.' This is no exaggeration of the beauty of this lovely spot. A few years ago it was threatened with destruction, and the resolution of the Corporation of London to purchase the manor and preserve the woods was universally applauded.

The southern environs of Windsor are even more delightful and attractive than the northern. If I had to make a distinction between them—between what I have partially sketched in this chapter, and the glories of the Great Park, Ascot Heath, Cranbourne Chase, and Virginia Water,—I should be inclined to say that the visitor who is most interested in historical associations, who prefers architecture to landscape, while admiring both, will find more to satisfy him on the northern side of Windsor than the southern, although the latter district must ever be reckoned in pure landscape one of the richest in England.

X.

The Great Park—The Long Walk—The Statue of George III.—View from Snow Hill—The Trees—Cumberland Lodge—The Sandbys—Virginia Water—The Ruins—Belvidere Wood—Bishopsgate—Holloway College—Ascot—The Church—The Race-Course—The Southern Environs of Windsor.

THE chief glory of Windsor after the Castle is the Great Park. It lies wholly to the south; for, though the ancient honour of Windsor extended beyond the Thames far to the north, and much of it was forest, since the seventeenth century only what we know as the Great Park and the open woodlands adjoining in Berkshire and Surrey have remained to tell of the time when the Norman kings could hunt over a tract one hundred and eighty miles in circuit. In 1607, Norden made a map of the Great Park for King James I., when the circuit was given as about seventy-seven miles. This included what remained of the forest, but the Park itself was rather smaller than at present. Until the last century the Castle may be said to have stood in the town of Windsor, and to have been almost surrounded by houses. At one side was the small enclosed tract, for garden and pleasure-ground of the Little Park. There was a wide gulf between this and the Great Park, but the town and Castle were connected with it by what is now the Long Walk, which, as we saw in the last chapter, was projected, if not actually completed, in the reign of Charles II. In 1670, Evelyn visited Windsor, and describes the King as busied with the planting of rows of trees. Mr. Menzies, whose history of the 'Great Park and Forest' is the best authority on the subject, conjectures that the idea of planting avenues of elms was borrowed about this time from France, and doubts that the elm is a native English tree, although, from the ease with which it is transplanted, and the great quantity of brushwood which it yields without injury, it very early became a favourite in this country. He further observes, as having a probable bearing on the date of the introduction of this tree, 'that while oak, ash, fir, yew, box, and other indigenous trees, have names of different origin, elm—like plane, poplar, pine, chestnut, and other trees of undoubted southern origin—has a Latin name.'

It is now as nearly as possible two hundred years since the Long Walk was planted. The distance from the Castle to Snow Hill, on which

WINDSOR PARK.

Westmacott's statue of George III. stands, is two miles and three quarters. As we see it now, there are, unfortunately, great gaps in the rows of elms, but there were originally 1652 trees placed ten feet apart. This, in the opinion of Mr. Menzies, is too close for the health of the trees; and he also thinks that the hundred and fifty feet, which is the width of the Avenue, is not sufficient for its great length. The soil has not suited the elms in some places, and young English oaks have had to be substituted. Charles had to purchase some intervening fields in order to carry his Avenue across to the Great Park. It seems probable that the avenue was completed in his time, although tradition has connected the name of William III. with the work. No doubt he may have renewed single trees, and there are slight differences of age observable among those at the southern end.

To the left, or east, side of the avenue there are still very easily distinguished interruptions in the continuity of the Park. We can make out the gilt cross of the Mausoleum, gleaming among the trees of Frogmore, and a little further we pass by the Shaw Farm. These, and other distinct holdings on both sides, are now in the hands of the Crown, but from the Castle to the Double Gates we do not know what is park, what is public road, what is enclosed farm—the Long Walk runs through all obstacles; and it is by a series of improvements carried on during many generations that the fields on either side have been gradually cleared of houses, laid down in grass, planted, and made more and more park-like in character. The result is eminently satisfactory. Looking from George the Fourth's Gateway towards the statue which he placed on Snow Hill in honour of 'the best of fathers,' we can follow an uninterrupted vista, such as long ages of wealth and care could alone produce. Once we are within the Great Park at the Double Gates the character of the landscape changes considerably. For one thing, it is much more hilly and more open; but what strikes the eye before all is the number of magnificent old trees, chiefly oak and beech, which are dotted here and there—sometimes singly, sometimes in a row of three or four together, and sometimes forming thick clumps of the deepest shade. With these there is, of course, a great deal that is comparatively new, but the plantations have been for so many ages the objects of constant solicitude, that trees suitable to every situation and to every kind of

THE LONG WALK.

soil have been gradually selected, until the whole is well-nigh perfect.

Standing at the statue, and looking towards the Castle and town, the view seems to be only bounded by the atmospheric influence. Distant objects come in and go out: the sunshine flickers a moment on a red roof at Eton, and transfers its smiles to a pinnacle of St. George's Chapel. Sometimes the town, and the battlements, and the trees below, and the wooded hills beyond the river, are massed together in a deep blue haze, while the Round Tower catches a ray and comes out clear and full with the Royal Standard floating above it. We have no corresponding expression in English to the American term 'Spread-eagle-ism'—something like it is wanted to describe the feeling with which most of us look through the Long Walk from Snow Hill. I have had the same sensation at one other place only on the earth's surface, and that is Gibraltar. Malta is beautiful, Aden is grim and majestic, one has a thrill of pride at the first sight of the triangular patch of white sand which distinguishes Trafalgar from the neighbouring headlands; but only Windsor and Gibraltar excite in the breast of the average Englishman that throb of pride and admiration which we may label 'British-Lion-ism.'

One reason is the extraordinary beauty of both places. Our concern here is with Windsor only, but a little of the same verdure and the same success in landscape-gardening has followed Tommy Atkins to Gibraltar. I have heard captious critics complain that there is no background of lofty rocks and snow-clad peaks at Windsor. It is difficult to listen with patience to such opinions. One of the charms of the view is that there are no cliffs or glaciers, but Windsor on its hill

> 'Doth itself present
> With such an easy and unforced ascent
> That no stupendous precipice denies
> Access, no horror turns away our eyes:
> But such a rise as doth at once invite
> A pleasure and a reverence from the sight.'

Everything is sweet and soft, green and grey, full of broad sunshine and deep shadow, full of old age and the echoes of long time, and full, also, of freshness and youth—young trees growing up to be to our children what the old ones have been to us; young deer bounding through the glades as their ancestors bounded when King William loved them 'as if he

WINDSOR PARK.

had been their father.' The combination of architectural magnificence and arboreal luxuriance, of venerable memories with the realities of modern and actual regal state, is very powerful; and the visitor who once sits down on the rough stones under the statue will probably linger long in contemplation, while unaccustomed thoughts crowd into his mind.

The most remarkable trees in the Great Park have been described by Mr. Menzies. There are finer oaks and beeches in several other English parks, but nowhere else is there such a profusion of the best kind of timber, or on the other hand so wide a variety of different species. Whatever was rarest came to Windsor in times past, and comes still. Pines from the Himalayas and the Andes, larches and birches from Scandinavia, chestnuts from Spain, and cedars from Syria, are growing beside our native English trees, affording endless changes of foliage in the same vast 'contiguity of shade.'

The oldest trees described by Mr. Menzies are scattered about in different parts of the Park, and some of the best of them are, strictly speaking, outside its boundaries, in Cranbourne Chase and the Belvidere Wood. A pollard oak at Forest Gate may be as much as eight hundred years old. It measures twenty-six feet ten inches at the height of five feet from the ground. A very fine tree, measuring one hundred feet in height, is near the Royal Lodge, a little south of the statue. It is comparatively young, having not yet reached its second century. Three trees in Cranbourne Chase are called after Queen Anne, Queen Charlotte, and Queen Victoria. They are all oaks, and the probable age of the oldest is four hundred and fifty years. Some of the most beautiful trees are beeches. One near Virginia Water and another at Ascot Gate are mentioned by Mr. Menzies as being probably eight hundred years old. Some magnificent examples are near Cumberland Lodge.

I have had occasion to mention Cumberland Lodge more than once. It stands on ground which commands a beautiful view, and seems from the old drawings that have come down to us to have been a very handsome red brick house in Wren's best domestic style. It has been altered and partially burnt and Gothicised until there is very little of the original work left. So, too, the favourite residence of George IV., which stood very near, has almost entirely disappeared, and the Chapel has become a rather pretty little modern church for the use of people who live in the Great Park. The avenues of oaks near it date from the time of Charles II.

The immediate neighbourhood to the southward

CUMBERLAND LODGE.

abounds in evidences of its ancient sylvan character. There are broad stretches of open heath, as at Ascot and Chobham, alternating with shady woods, as at Swinley and the outskirts of Sandhurst; but the most beautiful feature, and perhaps the best known only dates from the end of the last century. When William, Duke of Cumberland, the hero of Culloden, was Ranger of the Park, he had the good fortune to secure as deputy Thomas Sandby, the brother of

Paul Sandby, who is well known as one of the fathers of English water-colour art. To this circumstance is owing the existence of Virginia Water, an artificial lake excelled only in size by that at Blenheim. Paul Sandby's views of the Castle as it was before Wyatville are valuable in showing us the state into which it had fallen as well as from their great artistic merit. His brother showed equal powers in landscape-gardening, and was also no mean artist. Many of his drawings are in the Queen's Library. By judiciously damming a little stream, and by planting out obnoxious roads and houses, the utmost appearance of extent was secured, and the effect was heightened by the construction of a waterfall, which was completed in 1790, shortly before the death of the second Duke. George IV. was fond of fishing in the lake, and constructed various edifices by way of ornament on the shores. Among these the most singular are the ruins. They really consist of a number of columns and capitals which were brought, according to Mr. Taylor, from Tripoli, in Africa, by Sir Frederic Ponsonby, when he was the Governor of Malta. Unfortunately, although they are all genuine antiquities of the Roman period, they come from two or three different buildings, and as now set up the capitals do not always belong to the shafts and the bases. Several inscriptions have been found among them which betray a very late period. One of them relates to the worship

ARTIFICIAL RUINS AT VIRGINIA WATER.

of Serapis, and another is the epitaph of Domitia Rogata, the wife of Julius Cethegus, who died at the age of twenty-three.

Close to Virginia Water, but across the road, is the Belvidere Wood, otherwise known as Shrubb's Hill, from which a beautiful view can be obtained, extending, it is said, into seven counties. The tower is not very worthy of the place, but was built on the site of a summer-house by George IV., and mounts some brass cannon, which are said to have been used at the battle of Culloden, and are certainly of about that date.

From Virginia Water eastward, although there is not much Crown land there are so many large and well-wooded parks that the roads constantly run under arching trees, and the undulating character of the country adds to its attractions. The view from Cooper's Hill was celebrated at the very beginning of the last century by Sir John Denham in a poem, some lines of which are still often quoted, as where he apostrophises the Thames:—

> 'O could I flow like thee, and make thy stream
> My great example, as it is my theme:
> Tho' deep yet clear, tho' gentle, yet not dull,
> Strong without rage, without o'erflowing full!'

Englefield Green, close by, leads to the Bishopsgate, within which is much of the best wooded scenery of the Great Park. It is impossible in any description to do justice to the wilderness of bracken, to the spreading shade of the ancient beeches, to the glancing of the light through the branches, to the birds and animals which inhabit the thickets, from the great red deer to the squirrel, from the ringed pheasant to the wood-pecker. Every little dell seems to teem with life, and the naturalist who wishes to observe the habits of wild animals cannot fail to enjoy himself to the utmost here.

In the neighbourhood of Englefield Green is to be seen the great College erected by the late Mr. Holloway. The situation is admirably chosen, but of the building it is not possible to say much. The best side is that away from the road, where the architect has had to depend more upon proportion than upon ornament to obtain an effect. Nearer to Virginia Water is the Sanatorium erected by the same gentleman, a less ornamental, but in many respects a much more pleasing building.

Of late years a great deal of Crown land on this side of Windsor has been let for the erection of villas. It is to be hoped that too much will not be thus employed, as the rural character of such places as Ascot is very easily lost and can never be recovered. Several roads lead to Ascot Heath from the Park, and from one of them the 'Golden Gates' open directly on the end of 'the new mile' of the race-course. By these gates, which are of cast-iron, elaborately gilt, as the name implies, the royal carriages approach the Grand Stand at the annual races. The course continues across another road and up the hill, skirting the eastern side of the open heath. Along a considerable part of its length it is lined with stands—large and elaborate buildings—which are empty and useless for three hundred and sixty days out of three hundred and sixty-five! In the race week there is a stampede of the inhabitants, and every house that can be made available is let, in most cases at an enormous price, for the few festal days. There are not, so far, a great number of such houses, and Ascot, considering its fame, is a very small place. The town, if a town is sought, consists of a row of irregular houses along one side of the London road, terminating in a new and very handsome red brick church. No visitor to Ascot should omit to see the interior, which has been decorated in a very harmonious and pleasing manner, with paintings on the bare brickwork. There is a kennel for Her Majesty's staghounds near the Heath, and in the magnificent expanse of Swinley Wood, about a mile off south-

DEER IN WINDSOR PARK.

west, are paddocks for the red deer selected annually to be hunted. Some very fine trees are near the paddocks, and the whole wood repeats in many places the glories of the Great Park. There are no training stables at Ascot, where, in fact, a racehorse is never seen except in June; and but for its annual carnival it would be impossible to find, so near London, a place so entirely bucolical, with its endless woods, its wide heath, and its shady, quiet roads.

The races were, like Virginia Water, a hobby of the two Dukes of Cumberland. Mr. Arthur Dasent has been at the trouble of unravelling their history in the pages of the Parish Magazine, and from his researches we learn that the race week was not established by the first Duke, but grew out of that very ancient institution—the Royal Hunt. In 1727 there was a race on Ascot Heath 'for such horses as had in the preceding season carried their owners to the death of a leash of stags in Windsor Forest.' The present course was laid out in 1751 or 1752. In the latter year the Duke of Cumberland ran a horse named Button, being the first time he was concerned in the meeting. Thomas Sandby, no doubt, it was who chose the place and direction of the course. In 1753 there were two meetings —one in May and one in August—and among the prizes run for was a 50*l.* plate for 'horses regularly hunted with His Royal Highness the Duke's hounds, or any real pack of staghounds.' The Duke had a large racing stud, and is always remembered in turf annals as the breeder of the famous 'Eclipse.' The second Duke, who was also Ranger of Windsor Park, was equally fond of the Ascot racecourse, and before his death the meeting was regularly established, and has subsisted ever since.

Although, as I observed in concluding the last chapter, there is not so much on the south side of Windsor of antiquarian or artistic interest as on the northern side, the few places I have mentioned will show how much there is of beautiful wooded scenery, of a kind to be seen only in England, and well worthy of attention, especially from the lover of landscape and the artist. No mere descriptions can do it justice, even the kind of justice that may be done to an old building or a picture. The charm consists in so many impalpable things, and depends on so many accidental circumstances, such as weather, that one visitor may be disappointed in what has raised another to the highest point of enjoyment. Nevertheless, given a fine day, and given an absence of fatigue, I think very few people will be found who do not count an excursion in Windsor Great Park, and the breezy open heaths beyond, one of the greatest of possible pleasures. 'Here,' as Pope sang in the reign of Queen Anne, in verses far truer in the reign of Queen Victoria,—

> ' Here hills and vales, the woodland and the plain,
> Here earth and water seem to live again,
> Not Chaos-like together crushed and bruised,
> But as the world harmoniously confused :
> Where order in variety we see
> And where, though all things differ, all agree.'

XI.

The Antiquity of Windsor Castle as a Residence—A Storehouse of Works of Art—The State Apartments—The Private Apartments—The Library—The Gold Room—Old Furniture—The Long Corridor—The Dining Room—The Drawing Rooms—Edward III.'s Tower—General Gordon's Bible—Conclusion.

ALTHOUGH, owing to various circumstances, some of which have been described in the foregoing chapters, Windsor Castle looks as if it had been built but yesterday, there are many remains in it of very hoary antiquity. Deep down in the foundations of the tower called after Edward III., and not there alone, but in various other places, are Norman archways and scraps of Norman masonry which carry us back at least to the reign of Henry II., possibly to that of the Conqueror himself. In the Lower Ward, the most ancient remains above ground are to be seen among the irregular buildings on the north side of the Chapel of St. George. Here, too, we see what all Windsor Castle was like before Wyatville undertook its 'restoration.' We can forgive him much; for though he destroyed the charm of patches of old red brick, of green ivy, of tiled roofs, and the occasional intrusion of a

'Queen Anne' cornice or a Wren pediment, and although he pointed all his masonry with a black-looking mortar which has a disastrous effect on the apparent size of some of his finest and stateliest

buildings, he yet made Windsor Castle worthy to be the chief residence of the monarch of this land. Still it is in these shady recesses, and in such nooks and corners as the Little Cloisters, that we seek for the evidences of antiquity and the materials for pictures.

In the front of a modern-looking house a built-up archway shows features which date from the thirteenth century, and it might, perhaps, still be possible to identify exactly the situation, if not the actual fabric, of the chamber in which Edward III. was born. The double rebuilding which the north side of the Upper Ward underwent, first at the hands of Wren and then of Wyatville, might have been expected to have left nothing standing of so remote a period. But a former chapter contained views of what is still the chief entrance-hall, and of an apartment still in use among the domestic offices, both of which are at least as old as the ancient Order of the Garter itself. Strange to say, the two great architects just named spared not only such chambers as these, but also the very ground-plan of what was then the chief or only residential part of the Castle. A 'restorer' of the present day would hardly have been so conservative. On the

WEST END OF THE INNER CLOISTERS.

ground-floor, all along this side, with Wyatville's windows and doorways, we come across carved Ionic

THE CLOISTER GARTH.

pillars, in Wren's best classical style, supporting some new wall in the State Apartments above, and within a few feet an arcade or a little piece of vaulting which must have been designed by Wykeham.

THE INNER CLOISTERS.

It is perhaps a pity, that while the architects of the seventeenth and the nineteenth centuries spared so much work of the fourteenth, they did not leave more of it visible outside. It is, of course, impossible that more than a very select few can ever be admitted to examine the courts and passages which form the foundations and ground-floor of the halls and galleries above. Indeed, I should have avoided all mention of them, only that to give a true account of Windsor Castle, and to convey a correct impression of its chief claims on our attention, I must remind the reader that behind the modern walls, under the modern floors, there are features of such antiquity that no sovereign in Europe lives in a house which has been so long continuously inhabited as Windsor Castle.

Partly, no doubt, from this fact, it results that in spite of continual alterations, in spite of the extravagance of one king and the neglect of another, in spite of the vicissitudes of time and the changes in taste, Windsor Castle is a complete store-house of rare, beautiful, and costly articles. In each age the best things have come here, the best workmanship has been bestowed on the furniture and fittings. It is often impossible to admire the taste or design of, say, a door or a pedestal; but if you examine the way in which the faulty design has been carried out, your criticism is turned to admiration. There are, for example, some tall candlesticks of *ormolu* in the Crimson Drawing-room. They date, apparently, from the time of George IV., and are in what may then have been considered a Gothic style. The 'Empire' feeling is very strong in the design, over which it is not worth while to waste words, as it is literally anomalous; but the delicacy of the modelling and chasing, the exquisite finish of the chiselling, the closeness of the fitting, are beyond praise. It is the same wherever the eye may happen to light. Whatever you see is the best of its kind, though the kind may not itself be good. As we go through the State apartments, for instance, we come to an object which people who know consider one of the wonders of the world. This is the Malachite Vase in the Ball Room. In design, and especially in colour, it is terribly displeasing to the artistic eye, which must speedily glance past it out of the window to the lovely landscape beyond. Yet in England, at least, it is the best of its kind. The State Apartments contain many other treasures. The tapestry—from France—is said to be unequalled even in its native country. So is the Sèvres porcelain. In some of the rooms all the picture-frames are by Grinling Gibbons, and the

Ante-Room is filled with his work. To the lover of carving this one chamber will be repayment enough for the exertion of a visit. There are no such Vandycks, either in number, quality, or historical interest, as those in the Vandyck Room. The equestrian figure of Charles I. is quite equal to that for which 16,000*l.* was lately paid by the National Gallery. Nowhere else can the greatest of portrait-painters be studied to such advantage. In the Guard Chamber there is a shield which Francis I. presented to Henry VIII. at the Field of the Cloth of Gold. Dr. Waagen, who cannot be considered a credulous critic, says of it:—' This is the work of Benvenuto Cellini; and the rich ornaments of figures, mosques, and arabesques, are, in invention and execution, among the finest that exist of this kind.' This is high praise. In the Queen's State Drawing-room the same learned writer saw 'a very valuable series of portraits by Holbein, such as no other collection in England can display.' They are now, as well as Quentin Matsys' *Misers*, in a more private part of the Castle. But the State Apartments contain numberless other treasures, and the visitor who goes to see them wishing at first that some more apartments were shown, comes

T

away wishing he could have seen all that was exhibited.

The fine statue by Mr. Boehm, R.A., which stands in the Grand Vestibule, is engraved as the frontispiece of this volume. It represents her Majesty seated, in robes of state, with orders, and the regal sceptre in her right hand. The left hand hangs down towards a magnificent colley dog, which reposes on the ermine robe at one side. The animal was modelled from 'Sharp,' one of her Majesty's especial favourites. The statue, which is in white marble, was exhibited in the Conservatory adjoining the Albert Hall some ten or twelve years ago, and was deservedly admired, both as an accurate likeness and as a dignified representation of the august sitter.

As with the apartments shown, so also it is with those which, though they are closed to the general public, are often seen by visitors who come to make special studies. The Library, for example, which has been, in part, already described in these pages, is full of wonderful art-treasures, the accumulation of centuries. When I first began to take an interest in such matters, now many years ago, I remember my surprise at hearing there was anything in the Royal Library. Every one knows that George IV. gave, or sold, the old 'King's Library' to the nation, and that it is now in the British Museum. But this Library was never at Windsor: in fact, the difficulty of removing it thither, and of finding room for it, was among the reasons for parting with it. It is not for us, who so largely profit by the arrangement, to grumble at it. George III. had, in fact, commenced the removal, when he was struck down with his last sad illness. Whatever George IV. may have thought of literature, even William IV., who would hardly from his nautical training have been suspected of much love of books, saw that a library, and a good one, was as necessary to such a palace as Windsor as its stable or its cellar of wines. He began to bring together the scattered collections at Kew, Hampton Court, Kensington, and other minor royal residences. The gathering was unexpectedly large, and unexpectedly good. There were, of course, great holes and gaps in it; but, again, marvellous treasures of art were discovered, hidden away in cupboards and portfolios. When Prince Albert, soon after his marriage, began both to make some arrangement of what had already accumulated, and also to allow liberally for the purchase of what was wanting, the Royal Library rapidly became worthy of the name; and not only, as I have said, do specialists ask continually for leave to visit it, but there are some departments in which it stands alone. Not to take up too much space, I shall leave lesser wonders alone, and only mention those things which, if you would study at all, you must study under the kindly and courteous guidance of Her Majesty's Librarian at Windsor Castle.

Chief among these are the drawings by Leonardo da Vinci. This great artist, as Waagen well observes, left so few pictures that we are dependent on his drawings for a true estimate of his genius. No collection can be compared with this except at Florence and Milan, the three volumes of which it consists affording 'the amplest view of the versatility of this highly-gifted man; for besides the usual subjects and compositions, portraits, caricatures, landscapes, studies of plants, &c., belonging to art, we find here drawings for a treatise on anatomy, far exceeding the usual studies of bones and muscles required for an artist, sketches for the sciences of optics and perspective, and, finally, drawings for hydraulics and military engines.' This splendid col-

THE STATE STAIRCASE.

lection appears to have been brought to England by Sir Peter Lely from the Arundel sale in Holland, and Charles II. was persuaded to buy it. Frederick, Prince of Wales, the father of George III., bought Dr. Meade's collection of original drawings by old masters; and altogether, when the idea of putting them in order was first entertained, some 15,000 works of this kind, of various degrees of value, were found to be in the library. The Michelangelo and Raphael drawings alone would be sufficient to make the reputation of an ordinary gallery. In addition, there is the well-known series of no fewer than eighty-seven studies in red chalk and Indian ink, by Hans Holbein, representing the principal personages of the court of Henry VIII. It is impossible to understand the work of Holbein without an examination of these drawings. Another valuable, though modern, feature of the collection is the Raphael Cabinet—a gathering of every engraving, drawing, or even photograph, which could be obtained to illustrate, as far as possible, 'the mental processes and modes of operation' of the great artist in the creation of each of his pictures. The death of the Prince Consort prevented the extension of the same instructive process to Michelangelo, Leonardo, and other great artists. The idea is a noble one, and worthy of imitation in all schools of art.

It must not be assumed that the Royal Library contains only prints and drawings. The illuminated manuscripts, both European and Oriental, are of great beauty, and many of them of great historical interest as well. The printed books are such as can be seen in no other private collection, for this must be reckoned as, strictly speaking, a private collection. Among the chief rarities may be mentioned the famous 'Mentz Psalter' of 1457, a splendid and perfect copy; a copy of Coverdale's Bible of 1535, a book so scarce that no perfect example is known to exist; and a considerable number of Caxtons, among them the only perfect copy known of the *Æsop's Fables* of 1484. In one chamber on the ground-floor is the royal collection of miniatures, comprising not only a large number which are of value as works of art, but also many which may be looked upon in the light of family portraits, some of which have descended with the crown for centuries.

Scarcely second in interest to the Library is the Armoury, and superior to both, in the eyes of many people, is the strong room in which the gold plate and jewels are kept. The same influence pervades both departments that I have mentioned as having been at work everywhere else in the Castle. For barbaric splendour nothing can excel Tippoo's jewelled peacock, except perhaps his solid gold footstool in the shape of a tiger's head, with teeth of crystal. There is a supply of golden dinner plates sufficient for a party of a hundred guests. A wine fountain taken from the Spanish Armada gleams on one side, and Flaxman's shield of Achilles on another. Tankards, beakers, épergnes, salts,—in short everything, down to a pair of bellows, that one can think of as ever having been made of gold, are to be found in this dazzling Treasury.

After all, there is something savage in a taste for mere gold and jewels which seems to communicate itself even to those objects which combine art and richness in the highest degree. I turn from diamonds and gold to buhl and marquetrie with a certain sense of relief; and as Windsor Castle contains some of the finest examples in the world of ornamental work in the precious metals, so, too, it contains what I cannot help considering some of the best specimens of the seventeenth and eighteenth century furniture, now so much studied and so universally admired in spite of all the preaching and influence to the contrary of the prophets of mediaevalism.

It may be worth while here to remark that when it is laid down as an axiom that a mediaeval palace like Windsor ought to have mediaeval furniture one cannot but assent. No doubt, as an abstract proposition it is perfectly true. But where is mediaeval furniture to be found? Not even Queen Victoria in the plenitude of her wealth and power can command the production of a morsel of English household furniture such as was used for, say, the royal nursery at Windsor when Prince Alfonso was born in 1272. No such thing exists: and we have, in illuminated manuscripts and sculpture, very meagre materials with which to build up any idea of what such furniture was like. Barry and Pugin had only the vaguest indications to go upon when they furnished the Houses of Parliament in what they believed to be the style of the Tudor period. I am not here concerned with the reason of this dearth of Gothic furniture. I merely state the fact because, though Windsor is essentially a mediaeval castle, though we may be sure it was as sumptuously furnished when it was first built as the

ST. GEORGE'S HALL.

time would allow, though some of the fourteenth-century chambers are inhabited still, and though, above all, as I have already observed, good things have in all ages gravitated to Windsor and remained there, no mediaeval furniture of a more domestic character than the Knights' Stalls in St. George's Chapel is to be found there now. But of the furniture of the succeeding period it is full, and especially of examples of the best French work. The wealth of cabinets in the Long Corridor is unapproached elsewhere.

It may be necessary before going further to explain what the Long Corridor is. When Wyatville took Windsor Castle in hand, the various chambers which look out to the east and south in the Upper Ward communicated one with the other in such a way that each room was a passage, and except by the staircases in the separate towers there was no other means of access. This was the state of the private apartments of the Sovereign when Pyne described the Castle among the *Royal Residences* at the end of the reign of George III. The inconvenience must have been great—so great, indeed, that, as we have seen, Queen Anne and her successors preferred to make their habitual residence in a small but comparatively more commodious house on the south side of the old moat. But Wyatville, by building within the courtyard a series of passages three or more storeys in height, united all these scattered towers and their suites of apartments, and made of the passage on the first floor at once a means of communication between the various saloons, drawing-rooms, and state bed-chambers, and also a new and magnificent feature of his whole design. The doorways between the Corridor and the old rooms pass through walls of enormous thickness—the walls, in fact, of the ancient fortress: here and there windows had to be built up, and other structural alterations carried out, but the inquiring archaeologist can still easily distinguish the old work from the new, and can trace out the forms of the old towers as they were before the new wall hid their features from the Upper Ward. The Corridor is no less than 520 feet in length, is well lighted throughout, and has been formed by degrees into one magnificent apartment, filled from end to end with treasures of art, bronzes, marbles, pictures, curiosities, and, especially, furniture of a variety richness, and abundance not to be surpassed. It is no museum; far from it. The objects we see are not

THE CORRIDOR.

obtrusively arranged. They are not classified or selected, but if the fortunate visitor who sees them lets his eye rest for a moment upon anything he will probably be led to examine it more closely; and, whether it is a painting, or a china jar, or a cabinet, or a casket, he will find it well repays examination.

The first thing, in a kind of vestibule, that will attract attention is Theed's semi-allegorical group, in marble, life-sized, of the Queen and the late Prince Consort. The attitude and expression, and the merit of the portraiture, are calculated to disarm the criticism to which so much modern sculpture is open. It is enough to say that the conception of the group is superior to its execution, but that the faces are life-like and affecting in the intensity of their expression. On the walls of this antechamber are portraits chiefly of those court officials who were most in the confidence of the lamented Prince.

The Corridor itself gives entrance to some of the most magnificent reception-rooms. Close to it, for instance, is the Dining Room, panelled and ornamented in white and gold by Pugin, one of his early efforts, no doubt, in what, later on, he called 'the Christian pointed style.' It is a bright, handsome chamber, with a fine view from the windows, in one of which is a vast wine-cooler of silver gilt, designed by Flaxman. From the Dining Room opens the Private Chapel, which also looks as if it had enjoyed the benefit of Pugin's care, and is a small octagon chamber fitted with pews. In niches are small statues, among them a beautiful terra-cotta, by Dalou, representing an angel bearing in his lap five children. This is a monument to the Queen's grandchildren, and was placed here in 1878.

Beyond the Dining Room, southward, are the three drawing-rooms. The Green Drawing Room, so called from the colour of the silk hangings, contains, besides some admirable bronzes and some fine buhl, the Sevres dessert service made and painted for George IV. It is arranged in glass cupboards round the walls, and would need more than one day for a complete examination. In the Red Drawing Room are portraits of the Duke and Duchess of Kent (Her Majesty's parents), and of the Prince and Princess of Wales. Here, too, the furniture, fittings, hangings, and carpets, are all of rare quality. It would be but too easy to dwell on the magnificence of every feature of these gorgeous rooms, or to linger in the other sets of chambers

THE GREEN DRAWING ROOM.

which open from the Corridor. Her Majesty's own apartments are at the south-east corner, and immediately opposite to them, in the corner of the courtyard, and over the Queen's Entrance Porch, is the Oak Room, now chiefly used as a private dining-room. Here, besides some not beautiful, though probably very valuable, examples of Gobelins tapestry, presented by Louis-Philippe, are pleasing portraits of the Queen, and of three of her daughters-in-law. The towers which look out on the Park are so spacious that complete suites of chambers are fitted in each, and each has its staircase to the ground-floor. One suite is shown as having been usually occupied by the late Duchess of Kent, another as that in which Napoleon III. and the Empress Eugenie were received. The corridor turns by imperceptible degrees till, passing over the archway which opens on the Long Walk—from the windows above which a beautiful view is obtained—we reach, at the south-western corner of the Upper Ward, the Tower of Edward III. and the adjoining turret, from which, and not, as usually supposed, from the Round Tower, James I. of Scotland could look into what was long afterwards known as the Maid of Honours' Garden. All these sets of rooms are furnished in a clean, bright modern style, without too much disguise of the old features where any remain, and all are filled with works of art, pictures, miniatures, and especially family portraits, of which there must be many hundreds. Among them some 'assemblies,' by Zoffany, representing George III., Queen Charlotte, their children, and their courtiers, give one a pleasant impression, both of the taste of the day and of the artist's powers. But it would take up as many more pages as I have already written to mention even what may be seen of this kind at a single visit, and I have not left space to do justice to the Long Gallery.

I have already mentioned the buhl. We saw lately what could be done by the French school of the last century in the Hamilton sale, and also, to a minor extent, in the Jones' collection at South Kensington; but there are some low cabinets, and also a pair of tall 'armoires,' at Windsor, that, judging by memory, seem to me very superior. They are not of enormous size, but are of superlative workmanship. You are surprised at their simplicity. The construction is nowhere concealed. But the delicacy and variety of the chiselling and chasing, which is evidently all by hand, is simply amazing. A very fine ebony cupboard, more than six feet high, is carved with allegorical scenes in low relief, in panels, and was presented to Louis XIV. on the occasion of the birth of the Dauphin. It is not known how it came here. I must pass by the landscapes of Canaletti, some of whose views of old London could have kept me all day, and the portraits, both in painting and in sculpture, of eminent statesmen. I pass by the bronzes of the family of Henri II. and the statuettes of Louis Quatorze; I can only name the triumphal arches made for the first Napoleon, in alabaster and gold, and the long series of historical pictures relating to events in the reign of our Queen, because I want space to describe what seemed to me one of the most precious things in the whole collection.

At the extreme end of the Corridor, in a deeply recessed window, stands on tall supports of wrought *ormolu* a crystal casket, whose history and origin are unknown, except that it is some three hundred years old. It is of exquisite work and exquisite material, and so clear that you can see through it like glass. Within is a white silk pillow, and on the pillow a little shabby book, open. Below, an inscription, newly cut on a gold plate, tells you that this is the pocket Bible of General Gordon, and that it was presented to the Queen by his sister.

With this touching example of Her Majesty's appreciation of what is best and noblest in her subjects, our brief survey must come to an end. Whilst it has occupied me, I have had occasion to visit Windsor over and over again, and at every visit something new has struck me, something interesting or beautiful which I had not perceived before. Waiting for the Chapel to open one day, my foot stumbled on the tombstone of Sir John Dineley Goodere: what a romantic story might be recapitulated here! Another day, I observed, close to the Lord Chamberlain's office, an extensive collection of fragments of carved stone some of immense antiquity. In the town I found a little street in which there was not a single house later than the time of Wren. At one corner in the Park there are ten or a dozen oak-trees in sight, all of them as old as the Norman Conquest. In short, the longer Windsor is studied it seems to grow more and more worth studying: the difficulty is to select; and just as the artists who have illustrated these chapters might, without exhausting the picturesque supply, have made twice as many drawings; so, too, in arranging these notes, I have had constantly to pick and choose what to put in and what to leave out. Both they and I have been indebted during the whole course of our pleasant task to the privileges graciously accorded to us, and to the unvarying courtesy, nay, to the kindness of the officials with whom we have been brought into contact; and not of the officials only, but of a wide circle of dwellers in or near the royal precincts, to whom we have had occasion to apply for information or assistance.

LONDON:
Printed by STRANGEWAYS & SONS, Tower Street, Cambridge Circus.

www.ingramcontent.com/pod-product-compliance
Lightning Source LLC
Chambersburg PA
CBHW022026240426
43667CB00042B/1195